HAWAI'I'S 'Ohana COOKBOOK

From Our Family to Yours

Edited by
Joleen Oshiro
and
Betty Shimabukuro

with photography by
Craig T. Kojima

recipe coordination by
Galyn Wong

Library of Congress Control Number: 2011934668

ISBN-10: 1-56647-953-3
ISBN-13: 978-1-56647-953-0

All photography by Craig T. Kojima, except where noted below.

Photo on pg. 157, 191 by Kaz Tanabe
Photo on pg. 90 © J. Franklin Willis
Photos that were submitted by the families:
Nishimoto family (pgs. 8-9), Kinnicutt family (pg. 18), Aoki family (pg. 22), Freitas family (pg. 31—bottom photo), Philpotts family (pg. 34), Furuya family (pg. 76-77), Domingo family (pg. 114), Cheng family (pg. 162), Shimabuku family (pg. 176), Vierra family (pg. 178), Ro family (pg. 180), Ogoshi family (pg. 184), Kodama family (pg. 186), Tanioka family (pg. 195)
Photos courtesy Mutual Publishing:
pg. 170, 179, 182-183, 188
Photos from dreamstime.com:
pg. ii © Denys Prokofyev, pg. iv © Mcarrel, pg. xi © Ingvald Kaldhussater, pg. 8 © Jaroslaw Grudzinski, pg. 29 © Angelo Gilardelli, pg. 43 © Tomboy2290, pg. 62 © Casaalmare, pg. 65 © Elena Elisseeva, pg. 117 © Picsfive, pg. 119 © Ljupco Smokovski, pg. 121 © Anton Gorbachev, pg. 177 © Le-thuy Do, pg. 202 © Irina Ukrainets

Design by Courtney Young

Fifth Printing, December 2012

Mutual Publishing, LLC
1215 Center Street, Suite 210
Honolulu, Hawai'i 96816
Ph: 808-732-1709 / Fax: 808-734-4094
email: info@mutualpublishing.com
www.mutualpublishing.com

Printed in Korea

Table of Contents

Appetizers

Main Dishes

Salads, Soups, and Stews

Side Dishes

Desserts

Remembering

Foreword

The *Honolulu Star-Advertiser* has always been aware of the strong connection between family and food in Hawai'i through our Today section. Its coverage of food every Wednesday is one of the paper's most-read sections, particularly when there are articles on 'ohana cooking. As well, the tabs and inserts by our food advertisers leading up to holidays emphasize what to buy for that important family get-together, with their ads often featuring 'ohana and family.

All who live in the islands know of Hawai'i's strong culinary tradition, and the word has spread well beyond our shores. Visitors come from all over the globe to explore the island's culinary tradition (whether it's called Hawai'i Regional Cuisine or Asian Fusion or Local Grinds). What may not be as well known is that the islands' culinary tradition is heavily family-based. Many of our good restaurants are owned by families using recipes that have been handed down from generation to generation. Many island chefs, some of whom are world renown, got their start in the family kitchen helping mom and dad or grandma or grandfather. And at island family gatherings, a major highlight is bringing, sharing, and enjoying food.

To celebrate the islands' culinary tradition and its ties to 'ohana, we asked our readers to provide their favorite family recipes. The response was overwhelming, with families gladly divulging secret family recipes in the spirit of sharing—particularly the memories associated with the recipes' origins.

Joleen Oshiro, Betty Shimabukuro and Mutual Publishing's cookbook editor, Gay Wong, took on the difficult yet enjoyable task of choosing which recipes to include.

In the end, *Hawai'i's 'Ohana Cookbook* became a document of the island tradition of passing on family recipes. It is as if we had a select gathering of Hawai'i's families at a collective dining table where great-great-grandmothers, aunties, and uncles shared the culinary wisdom from the faraway countries where the families originated.

We also discovered Hawai'i's most popular 'ohana dish. So many families submitted excellent recipes for Portuguese bean soup that we included a special subsection on this popular dish.

All the recipes and their accompanying stories reflect each family's unique history and identity. The recipes are as enduring as the people who brought them from other countries and cultures decades ago. And they remind us what a great place we live in.

So pull up a chair, take a seat, and dig in.

Dennis Francis
President and Publisher
Honolulu Star-Advertiser

Acknowledgments

Many thanks to all the families who submitted the recipes that fill this book. Their contributions and their stories helped us define the values of family and tradition so vital to our culinary heritage.

This project began with a call for recipes announced in the *Honolulu Star-Advertiser* on March 2, 2011. Submissions came by email and snail mail, providing us with a huge bank of choices. Our selections were aimed at providing a balance of ethnic favorites with all-American choices; a mix of sophisticated recipes with easy weeknight meals. In other words, an island-style mixed plate.

Next, several recipes were selected to be photographed. *Star-Advertiser* staff photographer Craig T. Kojima and his assistants, Matthew and Lynn Bowden, along with Gay Wong, Mutual Publishing's cookbook editor, were welcomed into 20 homes to capture the creation of each dish in pictures. Craig's daughter, Cleo, also came along to help her dad. While Craig and Matt worked, Gay would sit at the dining table with the families, talking story and learning more about the way each dish fit into the family history.

Mitch Wakuya helped review the recipes to make sure the ingredient amounts and cooking times were accurate. Dawn Sueoka served as copy editor. Erika Roberts was invaluable in keeping track of submissions and acting as liaison with the many contributors.

Also helping in various ways were Mutual's Richard Ahn, Jane Gillespie, Alfred Monico, Jordan Padilla, Leah Ramos, Justin Roberts, and Courtney Young, plus Mutual's 'ohana network: Michael Miyashiro (Rainforest), Malia Ogoshi, Mike Gentile, Kathi and Mike Nohara, Jeffery Lee, Mark Okumura, and Josie Duchstein.

Introduction

The foods that populate family dinner tables and potluck buffets are infused with more than secret ingredients and refined techniques.

Whether we realize it or not, they're fortified with memories in the making, of people dear to us and the traditions we share.

Perhaps this is why food is such a big deal in the Islands. Family looms large in Hawai'i, but it's not enough to gather with loved ones. We must also feed one another. That sharing of sustenance becomes part of our fiber.

I am fortunate to have many family traditions tucked away in my heart and mind. A dish of tofu salad, for instance, unleashes remembrances of New Year's Eve at Grandma Oshiro's house. With every bite of tofu, I can also recall Aunty Lois's chow mein, topped with shiitake, pork, carrots, water chestnuts, Chinese peas and lots of gravy. It shared space on the food table with Aunty Doris's baked ham, mac salad, and maki sushi, Aunty Margret's roast turkey with chestnut stuffing and Mom's lumpia and konbu maki. Not to mention her tofu salad.

Most importantly, I remember the seemingly endless laughter and song. My dad and his siblings were a happy, musical bunch. Late into the night, they played ʻukulele and sang Hawaiian songs. At midnight, Aunty Helen would pop open the champagne as they sang "Auld Lang Syne" and hugged each other, a rarity in our Asian family.

The last of those parties took place about 15 years ago. Today just a couple of the siblings remain. How precious those memories have become. It just takes some tofu salad to recall them.

I'm hardly unique. Everyone has such remembrances.

It is with this understanding of the deep ties between food and family that we thank the folks who shared the recipes that make up this cookbook. We know that each one is imbued with the love, support and celebration that families come together to share.

— Joleen Oshiro

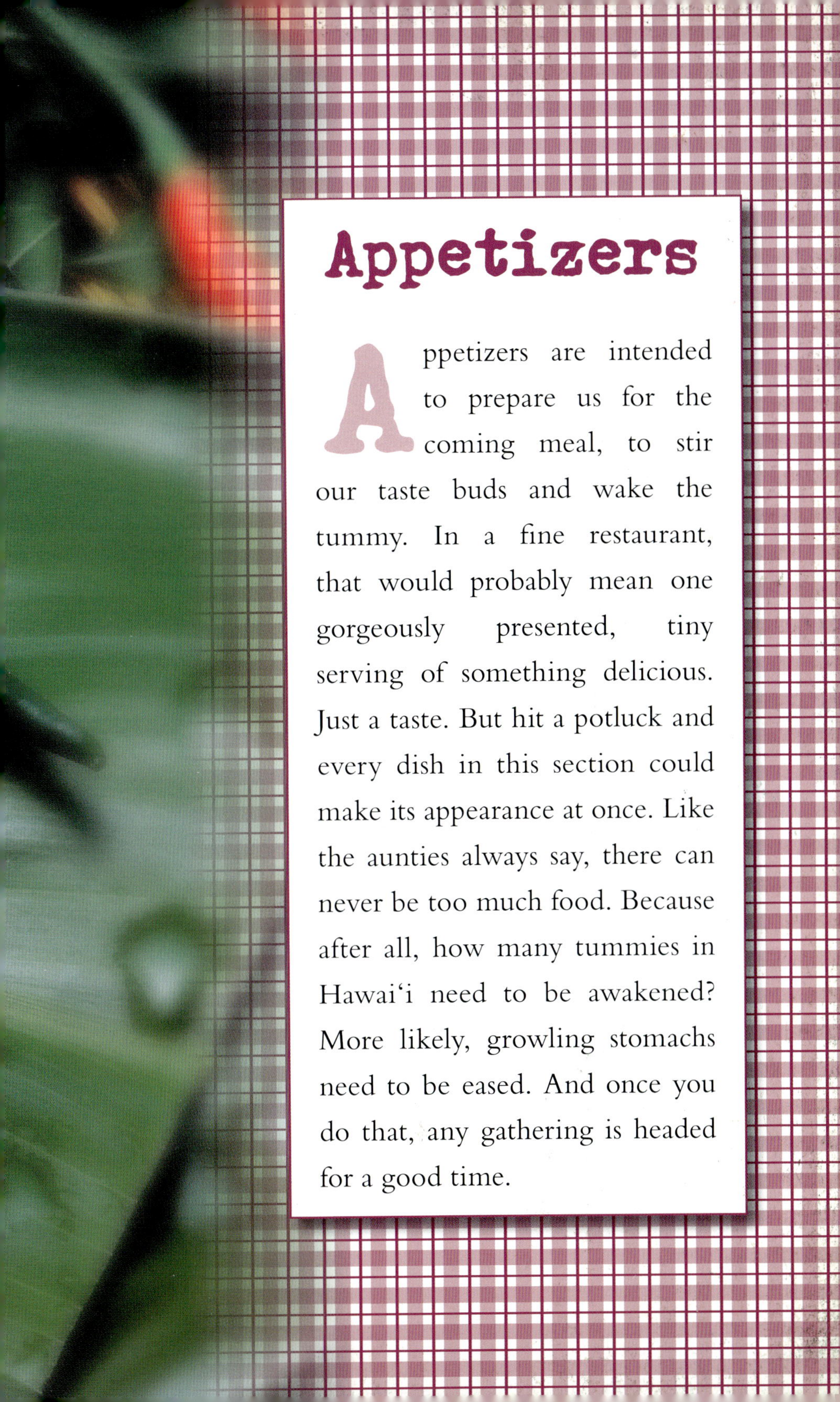

Appetizers

Appetizers are intended to prepare us for the coming meal, to stir our taste buds and wake the tummy. In a fine restaurant, that would probably mean one gorgeously presented, tiny serving of something delicious. Just a taste. But hit a potluck and every dish in this section could make its appearance at once. Like the aunties always say, there can never be too much food. Because after all, how many tummies in Hawai'i need to be awakened? More likely, growling stomachs need to be eased. And once you do that, any gathering is headed for a good time.

Scallion Pancakes
(Chung Yao Beng)

Submitted by Jamie Cheng

It is always comforting when my father-in-law fries something delicious in his wok, a masterpiece of welded parts that he fashioned himself like a Chinese MacGyver. I don't think I've ever seen him pick up a measuring spoon or use a kitchen scale. He simply uses his hand as his scale and a rice bowl as his measuring cup.

While living with my in-laws, I would come home every night to a delicious home-cooked Chinese meal. Things I never saw before in a Chinese restaurant. Healthy, delectable, colorful dishes that went way beyond the beef broccoli and shrimp Canton I knew Chinese cooking to be. Every night, around platters of chestnut chicken, steamed fish with ginger and hot oil, and choy sum, I would learn a little more about my in-laws: stories about leaving Guangdong Province in Southern China, moving to America and opening a Chinese restaurant, and raising four children.

He founded Kin Wah Restaurant in 1982 with his sister Jane and her husband, Kinsang Wong. They worked tirelessly, no holidays or weekends off. In 2000, he retired and is currently known as "Fire Dragon" on the badminton courts.

Chung yao beng, a northern Chinese dish, was one of the first that my father-in-law taught me to make. It was something he learned as an apprentice chef in Hong Kong and continued to prepare for his children and grandchildren in Hawai'i. Chung yao beng is sold by street vendors in Hong Kong, much like pretzels are sold in New York City. It is a tasty marriage of fried crusty exterior and chewy inside layers akin to flat bread. Kids, adults, gourmets, and amateurs all love chung yao beng for its simple preparation and tasty results. In our family, chung yao beng is a favorite dish that everyone can help prepare, even the kids.

recipe continued on page 4

Makes 5 pancakes

- 1-1/2 cups water
- 4 cups flour
- garlic salt, to taste
- 1/2 cup cilantro
- 1/2 cup green onions
- vegetable oil for frying

Mix the water and flour until a sticky dough forms. Flour your hands and a clean flat work area and knead the dough until the ingredients are fully incorporated. Cover and let the dough rest for 30 minutes.

Flour your work area and rolling pin well. Keep a bowl of flour handy to keep your area floured well so the dough doesn't stick. Divide the dough into 4 to 5 equal pieces. Take one of the pieces and roll it into a pancake about 1/8-inch thick. Spread 1 to 2 tablespoons of oil on the dough and sprinkle generously with garlic salt, cilantro and green onion.

Start at one end of the pancake and roll it in one direction until you have a long cylinder. Roll the cylinder into a coil or snail shape. Squeeze to bind the folds and then roll it out flat again. Continue until you've prepared all the pancakes.

Heat 1 to 2 tablespoons of oil over medium-high heat. Fry the pancake on one side until browned. Flip and continue on the other side until done (approximately 3 to 4 minutes on each side). Remove the pancake to a cutting board. Using a paper towel, scrunch the finished Chung Yao Beng to separate the layers and add texture to the pancake. Add more seasoning if needed.

Cut into triangles or strips and serve plain or with a dipping sauce of shoyu, crushed garlic, chili oil, and more green onions.

The pancakes can be prepared a day ahead of time and stored in the refrigerator. Oil a plate well and place the pancakes on the plate. Separate each pancake with a piece of plastic wrap (also oil between each pancake and the plastic wrap). Make sure all edges of the pancakes are covered by the plastic, otherwise they will dry out and harden.

Pork Patty Sliders

Submitted by Jim Nakagawa

This basic recipe came from my mother. It was originally a pork loaf steamed and served with won bok and gravy made with two tablespoons water and one teaspoon cornstarch. We are originally from Honolulu, but have lived in Hilo for the past 20 years. It has become a favorite of the in-laws whenever we visit for birthdays and other special events.

Serves 8

- 1 pound ground pork
- 5 water chestnuts, chopped
- 1-1/2 tablespoons shoyu
- 4 raw shrimp, peeled & deveined (21 to 25 count/pound)
- 1 teaspoon salt
- 1 tablespoon diced green onion
- 1 teaspoon sugar
- Love's dinner rolls
- Sriracha hot chili sauce

Mix all ingredients except Love's dinner rolls and Sriracha hot chili sauce. Form into bite-size patties. Fry both sides on medium heat in non-stick pan until browned. Let cool. Slice Love's dinner rolls in half but not all the way through. Insert one pork patty. Squirt a bit of Sriracha hot chili sauce on top. Ready to serve.

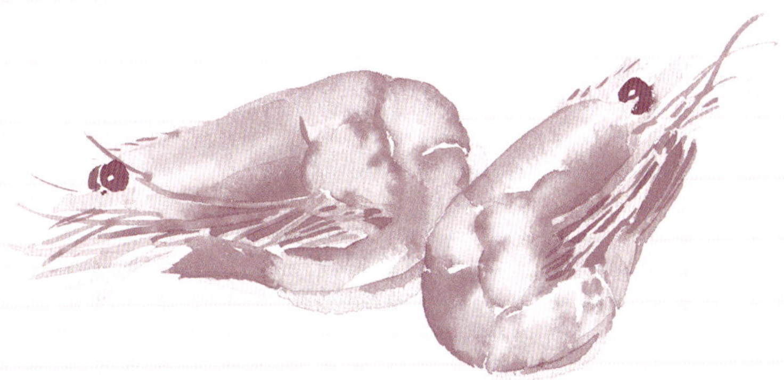

I'a Lawalu
(Fish Steamed in Ti Leaves)

Submitted by Larry Shigaki

My mom, "Aunty Mike," as everyone called her, was very popular. She was first on everyone's invite list. Her signature dish, I'a Lawalu, was always brought to the party.

Whenever butterfish would go on sale prior to the holidays, my mom would buy a couple of extra slabs. She would soak it in fresh, cold water, changing the water several times to remove most of the salt. Our job was to wrap the fish in ti leaves, creating a packet. It was a labor of love. The individually wrapped treasures were then gently placed in a steamer. Then, all we had to do was patiently wait. On New Year's Eve we would make about 150 packets.

At family gatherings, guests would quietly look to see if we brought lawalu. Before, when we asked, "What can I bring?" they would say, "Nuttin'." Now, they blatantly request lawalu!

Makes 12 packets

2 pounds salted butterfish*
3 ti leaves, washed and cut into 5-inch squares
6 Hawaiian chili peppers, sliced lengthwise
String

Soak fish in fresh cold water, changing water to rinse out the salt. Cut fish into 1-inch cubes.

Place cubed fish on ti leaf square with Hawaiian chili pepper cut side-down, making a package. Tie each package with string, securing with a knot. Place in a steamer and steam for 25 to 30 minutes.

For added flavor, include lū'au leaves, spinach, a slice of pork, bacon, or onion in each packet. Adjust the size of the ti leaves accordingly.

*substitute: salmon, moi, halibut

Konbu Maki

(New Year's Celebration Food—Chicken Rolled in Konbu Seaweed)

Submitted by Amber Nishimoto

This recipe came into the family thanks to my grandmom's good friend, Haruko, who shared the konbu-maki as a snack when all their friends gathered to get their hair done by their hairdressers, June and Kay. Grandmom brought some of the konbu-maki home for me to try, along with some packs of konbu and enough seaweed to last a lifetime, thanks to Haruko. Ever since, I have decided to honor Haruko and her generosity by making konbu-maki for every New Year's Day celebration, and it is always a family favorite!

Serves 24

- 3 pounds chicken thighs
- 2 packages nishime seaweed
- 2 packages kanpyo gourd strips
- 2 tablespoons mirin
- 2 tablespoons sake
- 2 tablespoons dashi powder
- 1/2 cup shoyu
- 1/2 cup sugar

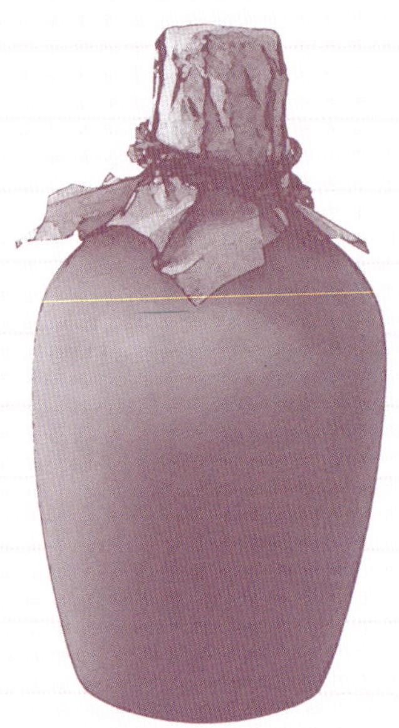

Place chicken in a pot of water and boil until cooked. Remove chicken and cool, then remove skin and bones. Cut chicken into 1/2-inch long strips. Place nishime seaweed in a bowl with warm water and let sit until rehydrated. Place kanpyo strips into a bowl with warm water and let sit until rehydrated. Cut seaweed into a strip 12 inches long. Place strips of chicken lengthwise along middle of seaweed. Roll into a long skinny roll. Using kanpyo strips, tie a knot every 2 inches.

Cut the seaweed into pieces with a tied knot in the center. Place pieces into a pot with the remaining ingredients and 4 to 5 cups of water, enough to cover the knots. Simmer until seaweed and gourd strips are tender and flavorful. Adjust flavor to taste. Cool overnight in liquid. Remove from liquid, enjoy!

Lomi Salmon Spread

Submitted by the Haynes Family

While attending a trade show at the Blaisdell years ago, someone at a food booth handed me a toasted bagel sample with some spread on it. I inhaled the entire piece in one bite. It was so yummy. I had to recreate that recipe.

Whenever I share this spread at a gathering, everyone thinks I chop, cut, dice, and slice all day, but it's all done in one little tub of lomi salmon. Gently fold in the cream cheese and there you have it. It's a winner every time and very easy to make.

My nana taught me that if you use quality products, remarkable flavors will be discovered.

1 container Taro brand lomi salmon
2 blocks Philadelphia cream cheese

Soften cream cheese, drain lomi salmon, and mix well.

Serve on toasted bagels or low-salt crackers.

Korean Chicken Wings

Submitted by Susan Yuen

As a child, Korean chicken was one of my all time favorite foods. Golden fried chicken wings that were lightly dipped in a sweet and garlicky shoyu sauce. Whenever my mom would make them (and she made them often), we would devour every last piece! The empty platter was a sure sign that it was a family favorite. In addition, Korean chicken was one of the first dishes that I learned to cook successfully as a young teen!

Serves 4

2 pounds chicken wings
2 eggs, beaten
3/4 cup flour
3/4 cup cornstarch
oil for deep-frying

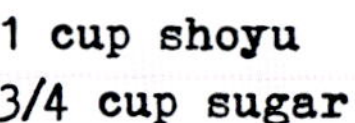

1 cup shoyu
3/4 cup sugar
1 tablespoon minced garlic
1 tablespoon sesame oil
2 tablespoons thinly sliced green onions
2 teaspoons toasted sesame seeds

Toss chicken in beaten eggs. Mix flour and cornstarch together and then dredge chicken one at a time in the flour and cornstarch mixture and shake off the excess. Deep-fry in batches in preheated oil until golden and cooked through. While frying the chicken, make the dipping sauce. Heat the shoyu, sugar, garlic, and sesame oil in a small pot on low until sugar dissolves. Remove sauce from heat and add green onions and sesame seeds. Dip the fried chicken in sauce before serving.

Aunty's Easy Crab & Artichoke Dip

Submitted by Micah Kukunaokala Richards

I learned this recipe from my Aunty, and it has been a winner among my friends ever since.

1 cup lump crab meat
1-1/2 to 2 cups mayonnaise
1 cup rough chopped artichoke hearts
1 cup diced Maui sweet onion
2 cups shredded Parmesan cheese
Pepper, to taste
Lemon juice, to taste

Preheat oven to 400°F.

Fold ingredients together in mixing bowl. Place mixture into small baking dish and try to get the mixed ingredients to be no more than an inch deep so it bakes evenly.

Bake for 45 minutes to an hour (or until golden brown on top).

Serve with either crackers or slices of French bread that are plain or lightly toasted.

You can also use mozzarella cheese and adjust a lot of the ingredients to your individual taste. It is a very forgiving recipe.

Main Dishes

Some dishes in this section originated generations ago and have been handed down, held secret until now; others have come together at the stove or in front of the pantry—the creation of a home cook's practical mind. A few recipes are a combination of both. There are old family recipes which hail from the likes of Laos, Okinawa, and Ka'a'awa. Busy moms and dads share their family- and budget-friendly dishes. Other recipes improvise on tradition, streamlining cooking duties with modern-day appliances such as the slow cooker. And many include the inevitable, favorite starch in the Islands—rice. There's nothing quite as inviting or comforting as a heap of pristine white rice sitting on the plate, steam rising like a veil over a hungry diner. Rice is the local palate's perfect accompaniment to any entrée, whether it's filet mignon or spaghetti and hot dogs. But sometimes rice can be jazzed up to become a headliner in its own right.

Whether old or new, this collection offers delicious ways to feed the family with recipes that dot the globe.

MOM

Pot Roast and Taro

Submitted by Annetta Kinnicutt

This old recipe was brought from Germany by my great-grandparents. The original recipe had potatoes, but I adapted it and added taro. We include this dish at every occasion and every get-together to celebrate them.

Serves 6

- 1 (5-pound) chuck roast (well-marbled)
- 10 carrots, peeled and sliced
- 2 large white onions, chopped
- Water
- Red wine (Burgundy or whatever you have)
- 1 box beef broth
- Bay leaves
- 2 tablespoons cornstarch
- Salt, pepper, herbs (your choice of herbs: rosemary, sage, thyme), to taste
- 3 large taro, peeled and cubed

This pot roast must be cooked in a pressure cooker for about 1 hour or in a heavy casserole pot in the oven for 1 to 2 hours at 350°F.

Brown pot roast on all sides in butter. Put everything in the pot with equal parts water, wine, and broth to cover the meat. Add a few bay leaves. Cover and cook for about 1 hour, until meat is tender when pierced with a fork.

Remove meat, onions, and carrots to serving platter. Cover with foil to keep warm. Mix 2 tablespoons cornstarch with a tiny bit of water just to moisten. Using a whisk to stir the gravy, add the cornstarch slowly a bit at a time while gravy is simmering. The gravy should start to thicken. Add more cornstarch and water if necessary. You must stir constantly to

recipe continued on page 18

prevent lumps. Add any herbs you like and salt and pepper. Transfer the gravy to a bowl for serving.

Taro:

Use regular Hawaiian taro, Lehua, or something similar. Peel and cut up in uniform pieces. Boil in water for about an hour, covered, for large taro pieces and check until fork-tender. Serve with the gravy and meat. Leftovers can be cut up and fried with cut up bacon and onions for breakfast with fried eggs.

My great grandparents and their six children (plus one son-in-law) pose next to their home on the Līhu'e Sugar Plantation in 1905. Plantation workers were provided minimal housing. In the foreground you can see shoyu tubs being reused as planters.

My great grandparents came to Kaua'i from Black Forest, Germany, in 1881, answering the call for workers. My great-grandfather began as a hired laborer but soon became a talented woodworker.

Sapasui
(Samoan Chop Suey)

Submitted by Jenni and Eddie Maiava

Every year at the end of summer we put on a community lū'au. We invite family, friends, and our children's classmates to come and learn Polynesian songs and dances. The sapasui is always a big hit—typically people come for seconds of that dish more than anything else. We also prepare dinners for our children's sports teams. We always cook "Poly" food, including sapasui. The athletes love it and ask for it every year.

Serves 4

2 small packages (2 ounces) bean thread noodles
1/4 cup vegetable oil, divided use
2 cloves garlic, diced
2 large carrots, peeled and diced
2 stalks celery, diced
1 medium onion, diced
Salt and pepper, to taste
1 pound of beef sirloin, cut in 1/2-inch cubes
2 cups water
1 cup shoyu
1 cup oyster sauce
1-1/2 cups cabbage, chopped

Soak noodles in cool water until soft. Drain and cut into 2- to 3-inch strips with scissors. Set aside.

Heat 2 tablespoons oil in skillet or wok. Add garlic and vegetables; stir-fry until crisp-tender. Season with salt and pepper. Remove from pan to serving dish.

Heat remaining oil and stir-fry beef until juices evaporate and beef is tender. Add water, shoyu and oyster sauce; bring to boil. Add noodles and cook 3 minutes, or until noodles are clear.

Return vegetables to pan. Add cabbage and toss, cooking until cabbage is wilted.

Beef Tomato

Submitted by Cassandra Aoki

My late mother-in-law, Fumiko Aoki, taught me to cook Asian-style food. This was the first recipe she taught me and it is a favorite of my father-in-law's, Wilfred. She would sometimes make it for potlucks when all of her four kids, their spouses and children got together for a weekly family dinner on Saturdays or Sundays back in the 1970s. Now, my husband Alan Hadama, my daughters, Danielle and Chelsea, and my seven grandchildren enjoy this dish when we have a family reunion.

Serves 4 to 5

Marinade:

1 tablespoon cornstarch
2 tablespoons shoyu
1 teaspoon sugar
1 teaspoon sherry or whiskey

1/2 to 3/4 pound tender beef, diagonally sliced against grain
1/4 cup vegetable oil, divided use
1 half-inch slice ginger, slightly crushed
1 to 1-1/2 cups cubed onions
1 to 1-1/2 cups cubed green bell peppers
1 to 1-1/2 cups sliced celery
1 to 1-1/2 cups tomatoes, cut in quarters

Gravy:

1/2 teaspoon salt
1 tablespoon cornstarch
1/2 cup water
2 tablespoons shoyu
2 teaspoons sugar
1/2 teaspoon garlic salt, optional

recipe continued on page 22

Combine marinade ingredients pour over beef. Let soak 10 to 15 minutes.

Place a 3-quart sauté pan, skillet, or wok over medium-high heat. Add a small amount of oil and add ginger. Add beef and stir-fry until medium rare. Remove from pan.

Add more oil and stir-fry onions, bell peppers and celery. When half done, mix in tomatoes and beef. Cook 2 to 3 minutes.

Combine gravy ingredients in measuring cup. Move beef and vegetables to side of pan, turn heat to high and add gravy mixture. Bring to boil 1 to 2 minutes, stirring constantly. If gravy becomes too thick, gradually stir in 1/4 to 1/2 cup water. Quickly fold beef and vegetables into gravy and cook 1 to 2 minutes more. Serve hot with white or brown rice.

Wilfred and Fumiko Aoki

Napua's Slow-Cooked Kālua Pig with Rosemary and Maui Onions

Submitted by Elizabeth "Napua" Poire

I've been working on this recipe for years ever since I discovered that the crock pot works just as well as the oven for making kālua pig. I have family in Michigan who use this recipe at least once a month. It's a big hit at the church potluck! The secret is in the liquid smoke and ʻalae. I add some of the cooking liquid to the meat just before serving to keep it moist. The rosemary and Maui onions give the pork a little extra flavor that you don't normally find in your traditional kālua pig.

Serves 6 to 8

- 5 pounds bone-in pork butt
- 1/4 cup liquid smoke
- 1/2 cup water
- 1 tablespoon dried rosemary
- 1/2 teaspoon black pepper
- 2 tablespoons ʻalae salt (red sea salt)
- 1 small Maui onion, thinly sliced
- 1 small head cabbage, steamed and shredded
- Additional ʻalae salt, to taste
- Steamed white rice

Place pork fat-side up in a 6-quart crock pot. Combine liquid smoke and water; pour over pork. Sprinkle with rosemary, black pepper and 2 tablespoons ʻalae salt. Place onion slices around pork. Cover and cook on low for 6 to 8 hours, or until the pork is very tender. Transfer pork and onions to a large pan or bowl. Discard the fat and bone and reserve 1/2 cup of the liquid. Using 2 forks, shred meat into small pieces or chunks. Add shredded cabbage. Pour reserved cooking liquid over meat and sprinkle with additional ʻalae to taste. Serve over rice and enjoy!

Simple Crock Pot Pig's Feet

Submitted by Steve Dung

I learned early in life that only moms cook good food. My mom, Edith Dung, was a stay-at-home mom and an excellent cook. She prepared all our meals. I was so spoiled with her flavorful dishes, I had to learn to cook! Cooking became my hobby. I liked to experiment with food from my mom's repertoire.

When I married Adelia, her concept of dinner was pizza and hot dogs. I was desperate. I experimented with recipes from friends, listened to how older family members prepared their sauces. Popo Lum, my son Spencer's babysitter, always made Pig's feet the old-fashioned way. It involved boiling and stirring for a few hours. Culturally, it's a dish for special occasions.

My son, Spencer, and daughter, Erin, have learned to appreciate good comfort food. It's what I do best. The following is a simple recipe for any time you have a craving.

Serves 6

- **6 to 7 pounds pig's feet**
- **2 (20.3-ounce) bottles black vinegar**
- **1 cup apple cider vinegar**
- **1 package brown candy sugar (wong tong, see note)**
- **1/2 cup light or dark brown sugar**
- **1 pound ginger (sliced or crushed)**

Parboil pig's feet 45 minutes, skimming impurities as it boils. Rinse clean and drain (this step can be done the night before).

Place vinegars and sugar in crock pot. Place pig's feet and ginger in crock pot. Cook on low 8 hours. (Hard-boiled eggs can be added in last half hour.)

Note: Black vinegar and brown candy sugar, or Chinese brown sugar, are sold in Chinatown markets. Adjust sweet-sour flavors to your personal taste.

Taro with Leftover Roast Pork

Submitted by Malia Ogoshi

My father was 52 when my brother was born. He lived as a bachelor for most of his life, and his cooking repertoire was pretty much limited to poached eggs in chicken broth and fried hot dogs. This dish is almost as delectable as its prerequisite dish, fresh roast pork. The first time he made it for me, I was blown away at how he finally cooked something better than my mom. I'm not sure why, but it's mandatory to cut the green onions in long-ish pieces (about 3/4 inch). If you don't have any taro on hand, you can substitute potato and you'll still thank me for sharing this recipe.

Serves 4

1 medium taro, scrubbed
1/2 pound Chinese roast pork
1/4 cup water
3 stalks green onion, cut in 3/4-inch pieces

Place taro in a pot with water to cover. Bring water to a boil then simmer until taro can be pierced in the center with a skewer. Drain, let cool slightly. Dice into 1x1-inch cubes.

Place pork in pot over medium heat and cook until fat is rendered and pork begins to brown. Add taro and stir. Cook 10 minutes. Add water and cover pot. Reduce heat to medium-low and cook another 10 minutes. Stir in onions.

Variations: Substitute 2 medium potatoes for taro and kālua pig or smoked meat for pork.

Roast Pork

Submitted by Chef Wade Tamura

Grandma Tamura was my inspiration for this recipe. Her home in Pearl City overlooked Pearl Harbor with all the Navy ships. It was always an adventure going to Grandma's. She would whip up my favorite dish, pot roast, as soon as she heard that I was coming for a visit. She would make enough to feed an army. Real local-style with plenty of food to take home. We had 'ono kine grinds for the week! I can still hear her say, "make sure you eat!"

She loved cooking lau lau with fresh taro, and her lū'au squid was to die for. When I asked for a recipe, her measurements included one handful of this and a scoop of that! And her techniques were unconventional—just mix until it looks good.

She cooked from the heart with lots of love, and her food was thoroughly appreciated.

This is my rendition of her recipe with a twist.

Serves 6

- 4 tablespoons black bean sauce
- 4 tablespoons light shoyu
- 8 cloves garlic, minced
- 1 teaspoons Chinese five spice
- 1 cup chicken stock
- 4 tablespoons sake
- 2 tablespoons Hawaiian sea salt
- 2 tablespoons hoisin sauce
- 4 tablespoons honey
- 1 tablespoons minced ginger
- 5 pounds boneless pork butt
- 4 tablespoons cornstarch

In a medium-sized bowl add all the ingredients except for the pork butt and cornstarch. Mix well and set to the side. Wash pork butt and pat dry, then slice in half, lengthwise. Place pork in the marinade and massage the pork. Marinate overnight in the refrigerator.

Preheat oven to 400°F. Remove pork and marinade from the refrigerator. Place pork on a racked roasting pan and add 1 cup of marinade to the bottom of the pan. Roast 1 hour. Baste with the pan drippings, then cover loosely.

Roast for another 1-1/2 hours or to an internal temperature of 160°F. Remove pork from the oven and let it rest for 10 minutes. Place pork on cutting board. Place the pan drippings over medium heat and bring to a simmer. Dissolve cornstarch with 3 tablespoons of water then add to the pan drippings. Stir vigorously so sauce will not lump. Slice pork 1/4-inch thin and top with pan sauce.

Fat Grandma's Gandule Rice
(Achiote Rice with Pork)

Submitted by Laureen Freitas

This recipe was taught to my grandmother by her mother, who was raised in Puerto Rico. My grandma married and lived on a plantation in 'Aiea. She never used proper measurements, which is why the ingredients indicate using a can to measure the water. This rice was always included on the table to celebrate special occasions such as weddings, funerals, baptisms, and Christmas. My mother never learned to cook Puerto Rican dishes, which made me bound and determined to learn all these recipes before they were gone forever. One day, Grandma talked me through this recipe over the phone. She told me to put in all the spices, and I thought she said add allspice. Needless to say, my first attempt tasted like apple pie. It took me three tries before I got it right! Her original recipe used only chopped pork, but I later substituted it with SPAM®, bacon and Portuguese sausage. Grandma, your legacy still lives on with every spoonful of your delicious rice.

recipe continued on page 32

Serves 8 to 10

1 package achiote beans
1 cup cooking oil
1 small onion, diced
1 can SPAM(R), chopped
1 Portuguese sausage, chopped
1 package bacon, chopped
2 bunches cilantro, chopped
5 cloves garlic, crushed
2 (8-ounce) cans tomato sauce, plus 2 cans of water
1 can gandule beans, plus 1 can of water
1 teaspoon salt
1/2 teaspoon pepper
1 tablespoon garlic salt
1 can pitted olives, drained
4 cups raw rice, washed
1 deboned, washed ti leaf

In a small pot, place achiote beans, cover with oil and bring to a boil. Strain oil into a larger pot then discard beans.

In a large pot, cook onion, meat, cilantro, and crushed garlic. Add tomato sauce plus the 2 cans of water, then the gandule beans plus 1 can of water. Add salt, pepper, garlic salt, and olives and continue to stir.

Add raw rice and bring to a boil, then lower heat and stir. Continue to watch rice but do not stir. Too much stirring will produce mushy rice. Cook about 30 minutes.

When rice is done, top with ti leaf and cover. The leaf will absorb any increased moisture.

Pork and Green Beans

Submitted by Lenora Ponce

I learned this recipe from my mother, who had been preparing it for us since I was a kid. My mom is now 90 years old and she no longer cooks. She said it's a very simple dish that she used to prepare every now and then. Whenever green beans were unavailable, she would substitute any vegetable in season.

Serves 8

3 pounds pork chops
1 clove garlic, minced
1 medium round onion, sliced
1 large tomato, sliced
1/4 cup shoyu
1-1/2 cups hot water
Salt and pepper, to taste
3 pounds fresh green beans (snip ends and French cut)

Cut pork chops into bite-size slices. Brown pork chops in a roomy pot or large, deep skillet. Add garlic, onion, tomato, shoyu, hot water and mix well. Bring to a boil. Simmer for 30 to 45 minutes until pork is tender. Taste and add salt and pepper if needed. When pork is done, add green beans and mix. Bring to a boil, cover and cook until desired tenderness of green beans.

Leftover Fried Rice

Submitted by Kaui Philpotts

Auntie Hazel Meyer didn't exactly cook "'ono," but whenever she attacked leftovers, she "ate 'ono." We could never figure it out. She didn't smack her lips, but when she ate anything, it looked better than what you were having. Auntie was widowed in her early 30s. From that day she never seemed the least bit interested in another relationship and instead became a companion to my grandmother. We loved her for her patience and tolerance. She read constantly, everything she could get her hands on, which was a lot at her job at the Wailuku Public Library. And best of all, she listened. She listened to everyone and never pushed her views on any one of us. When I was 20 and working in Wailuku, Auntie Hazel picked me up for lunch every single weekday and drove us to my grandmother's for leftovers. The conversation and aloha that flew around that lunch table has stayed with me my entire life.

Serves 2 to 4

2 to 3 slices bacon, chopped
1 egg, beaten
2 stalks green onion, chopped
2 to 3 pieces fresh ginger, peeled, sliced
1/2 cup or more leftover meat, such as sausage, pork, fishcake, char siu
2 cups rice, day-old
1/4 cup frozen peas, thawed, optional
2 to 3 tablespoons shoyu
1 tablespoon sesame oil
2 tablespoons oyster sauce
Pepper to taste

In a frying pan over medium heat, sauté the bacon until crisp. Remove and drain on paper towel.

Fry the egg, flipping over once, until cooked through. Remove and drain on paper towel. Chop into pieces.

To the remaining oil in the pan, add the green onions, ginger (which has been mashed using the end of a knife), and leftover meat. Sauté, stirring with a spatula, for about 1 minute.

Add the day-old rice, separating the grains, and stirring into the meat mixture, frying until heated through, 1 minute.

Add the peas, shoyu, sesame oil, and oyster sauce. Continue to stir the rice. Add the bacon bits and egg. Combine it all and adjust the seasoning to your taste. Add black pepper.

Serve in a bowl for a snack or light lunch at home. This is a great way to clean out the refrigerator. Anything goes!

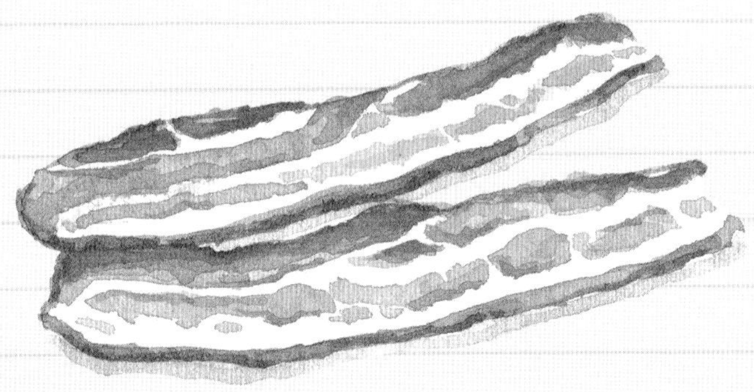

Chinese Sweet and Sour Spare Ribs

Submitted by Norman Len

My mother, Popo Len, was the master chef of the Len clan. She arrived from Canton, China, in the 1930s and spoke all dialects. Everyone went to her for advice.

My family owned Lenwai Store in Lahaina. Then, in 1948, we moved to Makiki on O'ahu and opened Punahou Market, the current site of PeeWee Drive Inn. Popo Len would cook lunch daily. She cooked ginger chicken soup, squash soup, lilyroot soup, and beef stew. The smells from Popo's cooking were intoxicating. Neighborhood businesses asked if she could sell lunch to them, too.

Asking Popo Len for a recipe was like asking for a beating. It was "a little bit of this, a pinch of that, or about that much." You had to just watch multiple times to see how much to add or what to do. This made it very difficult to learn and get it just right. I guess all great cooks are like this. Every time you asked a question, you got scolded, "I told you how many times!"

My wife was surprised to find this recipe in Popo's recipe box *with measurements*. Everyone who eats this raves about it. It's simply delicious and easy to make. I always give the credit to my wonderful mom. Thank you, Popo.

recipe continued on page 38

Serves 6

3 pounds spare ribs (usually found in slabs)
1/4 cup vegetable oil
2 slices ginger
2 cloves garlic, crushed
3/4 cup Japanese rice vinegar
3/4 cup brown sugar, firmly packed
1/2 cup water

Marinade:
2 tablespoons shoyu
3 tablespoons cornstarch
1-1/4 teaspoons salt
1 tablespoon sherry

Pineapple chunks (garnish)
Cilantro (garnish)

Wash ribs and remove gristle. Pat dry with paper towels.

Combine marinade ingredients and pour over ribs. Let soak 10 minutes.

Heat oil in saucepan. Add ginger and garlic. Add ribs and brown. Drain fat. Add vinegar, brown sugar, and water. Simmer 30 minutes.

Note: Ribs may be served with pineapple chunks and/or garnished with cilantro.

Mapo Tofu

Submitted by Sylvia Tomasu

I got this recipe from my mom-in-law, Susan Tomasu. I tried all kinds of mapo tofu from cookbooks, but my husband and children love this recipe the best. My mom-in-law used to cook it for family gatherings.

Serves 4 to 6

- 1 tablespoon vegetable oil
- 3 cloves garlic, minced (can substitute chives)
- 1 pound ground pork
- 4 stalks green onion, sliced
- 1 cup water
- 2 cubes beef bouillon
- 4 tablespoons shoyu
- 1 tablespoon sugar
- 1 tablespoon cornstarch mixed with 2 tablespoons water
- 1 block soft tofu

Heat oil and fry garlic. Add ground pork and brown. Add green onion. Add 1 cup water and beef bouillon, shoyu, and sugar. Add cornstarch mixture and stir until thickened. Stir in tofu. Cover and cook a few more minutes.

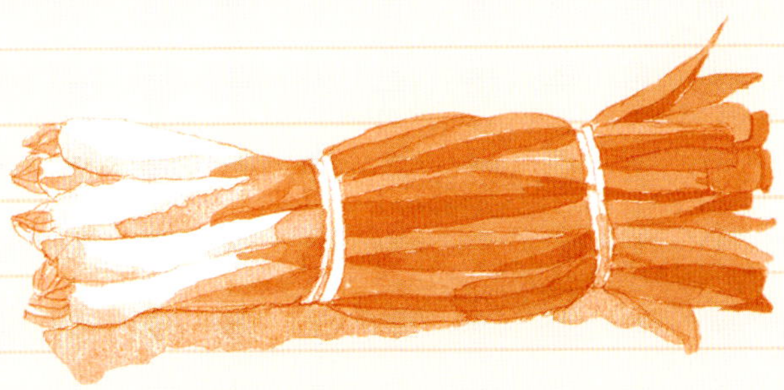

Cheesy Pizza

Submitted by Patsy Iha

I've tried different pizza recipes and they were not very good. I got ideas from those recipes, made adjustments with the ingredients, resting time, and baking time. I experimented with baking the crust before adding the toppings and it made the pizza excellent. This is the recipe I created, and it is now a family favorite. We don't order pizza because we can make it whenever we want to eat it. I buy the big bag of shredded mozzarella cheese from Sam's Club and keep it in the freezer. I have also made this recipe with my keiki cooking class. It is so simple that elementary school kids can make it in just 90 minutes.

Makes 2 (10-1/2-inch) pizzas

Dough:

1 (1/4-ounce) package yeast
1 cup warm water
1/2 teaspoon salt
1 tablespoon sugar
2-1/2 cups flour

Pizza sauce:

1 (8-ounce) can tomato sauce
1/4 teaspoon granulated garlic
1/4 teaspoon black pepper, optional
1 teaspoon oregano leaves
1 teaspoon sugar

Toppings:

1 pound shredded mozzarella cheese
Sliced ham, pepperoni, mushrooms, black olives, onion, bell pepper, tomato, etc.

Dissolve yeast in warm water. Let stand 10 minutes. Add salt, sugar, and flour; mix until cohesive dough forms and flour is absorbed.

Turn onto floured surface and knead 5 minutes or until smooth and elastic. If dough is too sticky, sprinkle with a little flour and knead it in. Return dough to floured bowl, loosely cover with plastic wrap and let stand 20 minutes.

While waiting for dough to rise, combine ingredients for pizza sauce. Set aside.

Preheat oven to 425°F.

Spread dough on greased cookie sheets using floured fingers. Let stand 10 minutes. Bake 10 minutes. Spread pizza sauce on hot dough and sprinkle with 2 cups mozzarella. Add toppings of your choice; top with remaining cheese. Bake 10 to 15 minutes more, or until outer crust is brown and cheese is bubbling.

Chinese New Year See Goo

Submitted by Malia Ogoshi

This recipe is definitely multi-generational—it was handed down from my grandfather to my mother to my brother then to me. My grandfather was an orphan who emigrated from China with his brother. He arrived with his queue (long pigtail) intact. I inherited the simple ceramic bowl he used to grow narcissus in every Chinese New Year.

My mom says the sliced arrowroot used in this dish resembles coins: a wish for prosperity for the coming year. We serve this seasonal dish with Mānoa lettuce as a wrapper for its bright green color and cup-like shape. I'm guessing the lettuce wrap was an innovation that originated in Hawai'i, since traditional Chinese dishes rarely use raw vegetables. My gung gung always had a garden in his backyard, so I'm sure he used home-grown lettuce.

Serves 6 to 8

- 1-1/2 pounds see goo (arrowhead) fresh or frozen (see note)
- 4 large pieces aburage (fried bean curd)
- 1 pound belly pork with skin, cut in 1/4-inch strips
- 3 pieces nam yue (red fermented bean curd)
- 2 tablespoons vegetable oil
- 2 cloves garlic, peeled and crushed
- 1 cup chicken broth
- 1 tablespoon oyster sauce
- 3 stalks green onion, cut in 1-inch pieces
- 1 large head Manoa lettuce, leaves separated, washed, and dried

Place see goo sprout side up on a cutting board and slice into 1/4-inch rounds. Pour boiling water over aburage, drain, and cut into 1/4-inch strips. Combine pork and nam yue, mix well.

Heat 1 tablespoon oil in pot over medium-high heat. Add garlic, lower heat and add pork. After 5 minutes add 1/2 cup chicken broth and aburage. Simmer 30 minutes, or until pork is tender.

In another pot, heat remaining 1 tablespoon oil over medium-high heat. Add see goo and sauté 5 minutes. Add remaining 1/2 cup chicken broth and cook 10 minutes, or until cooked through but still crisp (do not overcook). Add pork and aburage from first pot. Stir in oyster sauce. Taste and adjust seasonings (add water or broth if too salty). Stir in green onion.

Serve mixture spooned into lettuce leaves.

Note: See goo is sold in Chinatown markets during the weeks leading up to Chinese New Year. It is about the size of a ping pong ball, pale tan, with a sprout-like top. Buy firm, unblemished specimens. Wash, then trim off stem end, leaving sprout end intact. Carve the thin skin from the "equator" in one strip if possible. No need to remove all the skin. Frozen see goo is also available in Chinatown year round.

Foo Chuck with Squid

Submitted by Jody Domingo

This recipe has been passed down from my husband Robert's uncle, Aeko Jones. For many people living in Ka'a'awa, right across the street from the beach, fishing, and squidding were favorite pastimes. The bounty from the sea was plentiful. I remember him always preparing lots of fried fish, dried squid, poke, and many other dishes using seafood harvested from the ocean. When the tide was very, very low, the reef was exposed—ideal for squidding. My husband's family would hurry to gather squidding equipment, which included spears, tabis or old tennis shoes and, if you were lucky, a squid box. My husband and I liked to follow Uncle Aeko because he would magically make the water turn very glassy by sprinkling a few drops of cooking oil in the water.

Usually, Uncle Aeko would catch the most squid. He would string them on a wire coat hanger, which had been opened up and then closed again. About six squid could fit on a hanger depending on their size. He would place them in a large deep pot or bucket, sprinkle a couple handfuls of Hawaiian rock salt on them, and pound them. He did this by holding the loop of the coat hanger and banging them in an up and down manner against the bottom of the container. This would continue vigorously for at least 20 minutes or until the bottom of the squid's legs started to curl, which meant that the squid was tenderized. After rinsing off the salt and slime, he would remove the beak and ink bag. If it was a nice sunny day, he would hang the squid outstretched on a clothesline or put them in a drying box. Or, he would finely chop them with kukui nut and seaweed to eat raw.

Uncle Aeko worked for the City and County road crew and would prepare this dish at family gatherings. Today, it is rare that you can find squid in our ocean, but when one is given to us, I like to prepare this dish. We also make it for parties and have prepared this for as many as 300 people.

recipe continued on page 46

Serves 4 to 6

1 (6-ounce) package foo chuck (dried beancurd sticks), Two Swallow brand
2 ounces black fungus (chien gee or wood ear)
2 tablespoons oil
1 thumb fresh ginger, smashed
2 cloves garlic, minced
1 pound pork, thinly sliced
1 pound fresh squid, boiled and cut into bite-size pieces
3 tablespoons oyster sauce
1 (14-ounce) can chicken broth
8 medium-sized dried shiitake mushrooms, soaked, rinsed and sliced
2 tablespoons cornstarch (mixed with a little water for thickening)
1/4 pound snow peas

Soak foo chuck in cold water until softened, at least 2 to 3 hours. Drain water and cut into 1-1/2-inch pieces. Soak fungus in cold water for about 45 minutes. Rinse several times and be sure to pick off any wood bits.

Heat pan or wok and add oil, ginger, garlic, and pork. Stir-fry for 3 to 4 minutes. Add squid, oyster sauce, and chicken broth and simmer for 5 minutes until pork is tender. Add foo chuck, black fungus, and mushrooms. When sauce comes to a boil again, add cornstarch slurry and snow peas. Stir until slightly thickened. Remove from heat, ready to serve.

Country Ribs

Submitted by Cynthia Rankin (Betty Min)

This rib recipe was given to me by Pam Baldwin, who I met while my husband and I were stationed in Korea. She told me she had the easiest pork rib recipe in the world—and she was right! You pour the sauce on a slab of ribs, put it in the oven and an hour and a half later you've got a great meal! The ribs were comfort food while we were living overseas, and I still make this recipe when I want something easy to make for dinner. Pam loved to cook for us and invited us over to eat her native Thai cooking (because her husband and son didn't like it!). I think of Pam and our time together in Korea whenever I make this dish.

Serves 4

- 1/3 cup water
- 1/3 cup shoyu
- 1/3 cup orange marmalade
- 1/3 cup ketchup
- 1 clove garlic, crushed
- 3 to 4 pounds pork ribs

Mix all ingredients and pour over ribs. Bake at 350°F for approximately 1-1/2 hours.

Baked Pastele

Submitted by Julie Robley

It took my mother three days to make her pasteles by the dozens – one day to cut the vegetables, one to cook the meat and grate the bananas and the last day to wrap and freeze the bundles. Our kitchen would be off-limits all day while Mommy did her thing. When I was about eight years old, she had me in the kitchen burning ti leaves so they would be soft enough, and tearing foil to the right size (we didn't have the pre-cut foil that we have now). Daddy would help by grating the bananas while she peeled. If we could get the banana leaf, she would wrap the pastele in the banana leaf. My job was to burn the leaf and to cut the string needed to tie it.

When I was in my teens, my job then became to help with the peeling and grating of the bananas, mixing the masa (grated bananas) with the salt and achiote, and burning the leaves while Mommy cut the vegetables and cooked the meat. Our work was accompanied by Puerto Rican music on our stereo to help pass the time. We'd make 8 to 10 dozen. Once in a while, if there was a really good sale on pork, Mommy would buy 1 or 2 and we'd make a couple dozen to keep in the freezer just in case someone visited and asked for some.

By the early '90s, Mommy's health was deteriorating and making pasteles for three days straight, while standing, was taking its toll on her. So, she decided to try mixing the masa with the meat and baking it to see if it would come out. And it did! Now, once the baked pastele was done, we could cut it into "logs" in the pan once it cooled, wrap it in foil, and put it neatly in the freezer. She'd often defrost it, cut it like meatloaf, and serve it. Or, she'd break it up and mix it in the frying pan for a different take on scrambled eggs. My brother would be creative and make an omelet out of it. If family and friends asked us to bring pasteles to their potlucks, it was easy to make a big pan where people could serve themselves by scooping out a serving rather than having to fuss and fight with the foil and leaves.

Serves 10 to 12

- 15 green Chinese bananas
- 3/4 cup achiote oil
- 5-1/2 teaspoons salt
- 6 cloves garlic
- 2 teaspoons dried oregano leaves
- 1 teaspoon pepper
- 2 pounds pork, any kind but I prefer pork shoulder or pork belly
- 1 cup chopped onion
- 3 stalks green onion, chopped
- 2 bunches cilantro, chopped
- 1 (8-ounce) can tomato sauce
- 4 to 6 Hawaiian chili peppers, chopped
- 1 (8-ounce) can pitted ripe olives, drained
- 4 ti leaves, cleaned and deboned
- Heavy duty foil

Peel bananas and grate, soaking in cold water until all are grated. If the grated bananas are not soaked, they will turn black and dry out. Finely grate bananas into a large bowl. Stir in 1/2 cup achiote oil and 3 teaspoons of the salt. Mix well. Cover and set aside.

With a mortar and pestle, grind garlic, oregano, pepper, and remaining salt. Set aside.

Cut pork into small pieces. In a pot, heat 3 tablespoons achiote oil. Brown pork with 1 tablespoon of the garlic mixture; cook pork about 15 minutes.

Add onion, green onion, and cilantro. Cover and cook 10 minutes. Stir in tomato sauce, chili peppers, and olives. Cover and simmer on low 1 hour.

Note: Achiote oil can be purchased in most grocery stores. To make your own, simmer 1 cup vegetable oil and 1 cup ahiote (annatto) seeds on low heat. Stir constantly until dark red. If boiled too quickly, the seeds will burn and the oil will turn clear.

Pre-heat oven to 450°F. Oil a 9x13x2-inch baking pan with 1 tablespoon achiote oil. Lay 2 ti leaves on the bottom of the baking pan.

Combine banana and pork mixtures. Put this into the prepared pan. Cover with the remaining 2 ti leaves. Seal well with heavy duty foil. Place baking pan into a larger baking pan and put into pre-heated oven. Pour hot water into the larger pan to a depth of 1 inch. Steam/bake for 2 to 2-1/2 hours, making sure the middle is cooked. Add water to a larger pan as needed.

Local-Style Barbeque Spareribs/Chicken

Submitted by Lorna K. Hu

My husband, Hayden's, mom, Irene Punohu, always prepared delicious Chinese-style spareribs for our family dinners at her home in Kalihi. She was a good role model and a self-taught cook. Dinners were extra special when our children, Rachel and Trevor, anticipated her spareribs that were made with her special touch. She was proud of her dish and willingly shared her recipe.

I love to cook. On one occasion, I found this spareribs recipe. I modified the recipe to include a few more ingredients and made it for a get-together. My mother-in-law enjoyed it, praised my efforts and even asked me for the recipe! This recipe has been a loving reminder of all the special memories and fun we have shared together.

Serves 6

5 pounds BBQ ribs or 5 pounds chicken pieces
Large piece ginger
3 to 4 cloves garlic
Green onions

Sauce:
1 cup white sugar
1 cup ketchup
3/4 cup shoyu
1/4 cup oyster sauce

Boil ribs with ginger and garlic until tender. Combine sauce ingredients and pour over ribs or chicken. Broil ribs with sauce until golden brown. If using chicken, bake at 350°F for 45 minutes.

Nam Khao

Submitted by Rattana Soubandith

The knowledge and cooking techniques of our mother's native country, Laos, and what was taught to her by her mother and grandmother is what makes this recipe special to our family. Every Laotian family has their version of this nam khao recipe, which is commonly made during special Laotian celebrations. My mother taught this recipe to my older sister, Phinoura, and my sister taught it to me. Food is a celebration of life, and we as a culture enjoy the process it takes to create a wonderful dish for our families to enjoy.

Serves 5 to 7

1 tablespoon vegetable oil
2 cloves garlic, minced
1 pound ground pork
2 teaspoons fish sauce (or you can use salt to taste)
1/4 teaspoon sugar
1/2 teaspoon salt
1/4 teaspoon black pepper
1 teaspoon oyster sauce
12 cups cooked rice (jasmine or long-grain), cooled to room temperature
2 cups grated coconut (available at Asian Market on Beretania Street; do not use young coconut)
4 tablespoons (adjust heat to taste) red curry paste (best is Mae Ploy brand)
4 eggs, beaten
Corn or vegetable oil, for frying

recipe continued on page 56

In a saucepan or wok, heat oil and cook garlic 30 seconds. Mix in pork, fish sauce, sugar, salt, pepper, and oyster sauce; cook until pork is cooked through. Let cool to room temperature.

Prepare steamed rice as directed by your rice cooker or package. Once cooked, set aside and let cool to room temperature or cook the rice the night before and store in fridge.

Mix cooled pork and coconut, then mix in curry paste. Mix in 3 cups rice and 1 beaten egg. Add remaining rice and eggs in that order until evenly mixed.

Form mixture into 4-ounce balls (a little less than tennis-ball size). Keep hands wet to prevent sticking. Heat oil to 375°F, using enough to cover balls. Deep-fry 5 rice balls at a time in oil until crispy golden brown (turning occasionally for about 5 to 6 minutes). Drain on a cookie rack or something similar and cool to room temperature.

Note: You can either continue with the recipe below OR freeze the rice balls in a Ziploc bag in the freezer for up to 1 month. When you are ready to use them, bake them frozen in a 375°F oven for 25 minutes, and then follow the rest of the recipe below.

When you're ready to eat the rice balls:

10 cooked Nam Khao balls (2 rice balls per person)
1/4 cup green onions, chopped
1/4 cup cilantro, chopped
1/2 cup ham, diced (the kind you would use on sandwiches)
Juice from 2 limes, to taste
1/2 teaspoon salt, to taste

Smash balls into small pieces (like fried rice) and mix together with the green onions, cilantro, ham, lime/lemon juice and salt to taste.

Poor Man's Paella

Submitted by Christine Watanabe

As a single parent of twin boys in Hawai‘i, making a special dinner without spending a lot of money was a challenge. My boys had seen a paella dish in a cooking magazine I had around the house, and requested that I make the dish for their 11th birthday dinner. Since saffron and some of the other ingredients in paella can be quite expensive, I created this version which I secretly called "Poor Man's Paella" that saved money and won their birthday hearts. That memory stays with me until today!

Serves 6

12 pieces uncooked shrimp
2 tablespoons vegetable oil
2 cloves garlic, minced
1 onion, chopped
2 pounds chicken thighs cut into 1-inch cubes
1 (10-ounce) package Portuguese sausage, hot or mild, cubed
1 (16-ounce) package frozen peas and carrots
2 (5-ounce) packages Mahatma saffron rice
1 (10-ounce) can chopped clams (keep clam juice)

Clean shrimp. Remove shells and place shells into pot with 3 cups of water. Boil for 20 to 30 minutes until reduced to 2-1/2 cups stock. Remove shells and set liquid aside. In a large skillet, sauté garlic and onions on medium-high heat until translucent, about 5 minutes. Add chicken and Portuguese sausage and cook until pink in chicken is gone, about 5 to 7 minutes. Add peas and carrots to skillet, stir, then add rice, clam juice, and shrimp shell stock. Bring to boil, cover, then simmer for 20 minutes. Remove cover, add shrimp to top of pan and place under broiler for 3 to 5 minutes until shrimp is pink and edges are crispy. Remove from broiler and let stand for 5 minutes before serving.

Note: Use a large skillet with a metal handle that can go into the oven.

Tai Po's Minute Chicken

Submitted by Janice Chang

When my husband's grandmother came to live with us the first thing she did after coming home from Chinatown each day was cook. I helped and watched her so I was fortunate to learn the Chinese dishes she prepared. Tai Po's minute chicken tastes better than most Chinese restaurants'. The secret is the ingredients and it's finger licking good too!

Serves 6

Marinade:

2 pieces dried orange peel
1 (1-inch) piece ginger, peeled and chopped
3 cloves garlic, minced
2 tablespoons shoyu
1 teaspoon sugar
1/2 tablespoon whiskey

1 chicken fryer, cut into pieces
Salt and white pepper
1/4 cup cornstarch
2 to 3 tablespoons oyster sauce
1/4 cup green onions, chopped (garnish)
Cilantro (garnish)

To make marinade: Soak orange peel in water to soften; scrape off inside part of peel and mince. Combine with remaining marinade ingredients in large bowl.

Season chicken with salt and pepper. Add to marinade; mix thoroughly and refrigerate at least 1 hour.

Remove chicken from marinade and sprinkle with cornstarch. In a wok or skillet, heat 2 to 3 tablespoons oil over high heat. Fry chicken until brown, turning occasionally. Add oyster sauce and cover 5 minutes. Garnish with green onions and cilantro.

Chicken with Red BBQ Sauce

Submitted by Marbie McGillivray

This recipe is one of our family's favorites. Long summer days on the beach watching the green flash and having barbecues both in Guam and Hawai'i contributed to this 'onolicious sauce. My son-in-law summed it up when he asked my daughter, "Relish? Really?" and my daughter replied, "Have you ever tasted anything my mom made that you didn't like?"

Serves 5

5 pounds chicken thighs, boneless and skinless

Sauce:

48 ounces ketchup
1/2 cup sweet relish
1 teaspoon minced garlic
1/2 teaspoon mustard
2 tablespoons brown sugar, or to taste
1 tablespoon to 1/4 cup vinegar
1 tablespoon Worcestershire sauce

Combine sauce ingredients in pot and bring to boil. Remove 3/4 of sauce.

Add chicken to remaining sauce in pot. Return to boil and cook 20 to 30 minutes.

Preheat oven to 400°F. Lightly grease 13x9-inch baking pan. Add chicken and reserved sauce. Bake 40 minutes.

Hyotan with Gingery Garlic Chicken

Submitted by Cynthia Pratt

My mother, Lily Murakami, prepared this savory recipe when I was a child growing up in 'Ewa Beach over 50 years ago. When she moved to Makakilo in 1988, she grew hyotan in her terraced front yard and would prepare this recipe for my young children. My son loved this dish and never had to be coaxed to eat his "green veggies." The hyotan is soft and savory with just the right touch of ginger and garlic. It's a great comfort food atop a bowl of hot rice.

Serves 6

2 pounds boneless, skinless chicken thighs
2 tablespoons minced ginger root
6 cloves garlic, minced
1 teaspoon salt
4 pounds hyotan (long squash)
2 to 3 teaspoons vegetable oil
1/2 cup water, broth, or beer
Salt and pepper to taste
Green onions or cilantro, chopped (garnish)

Cut the chicken thighs crosswise into 1/2-inch thick slices. Combine the chicken, ginger, garlic, and salt. Set aside. Peel hyotan, scrape out most of the seeds and cut into 1-inch cubes. Heat oil in a deep pot with lid. Gently sauté the chicken on medium heat until done, about 5 minutes. Add water, broth, or beer. Cover and simmer 5 minutes. Layer hyotan atop the chicken. Cover and simmer 15 minutes. Stir gently, season with additional salt and white pepper to taste. Garnish with chopped green onions or cilantro, if desired. Serve in bowls with hot rice. Can substitute beef strips for chicken.

Mom's Baked Parmesan Chicken

Submitted by Lolly Saari

My mom and her sister were excellent cooks from Maui. Mom gave me this recipe in the 1970s and I've made this for family and friends—it never fails! My husband's friend came over for a Michigan vs UH game years ago and because it was also his wife's birthday, I was apprehensive—what should I cook?! I decided on this recipe and they still write to us about how much they enjoyed the "birthday dinner" with Parmesan chicken.

Serves 4

- 1/2 cup Parmesan cheese
- 2 eggs, well beaten
- 3/4 cup panko (Japanese bread crumbs) or cornflake crumbs
- 4 boneless chicken breasts, flattened
- 1/2 cup vegetable oil
- 4 slices Monterey Jack or pepper jack cheese
- 1/2 pound fresh mushrooms
- 1 tablespoon butter or olive oil
- 1/2 to 3/4 cup cooking wine
- Chopped parsley and lemon juice or lemon wedges, for garnish

Preheat oven to 325°F. Place Parmesan cheese, eggs, and panko in 3 separate bowls.

Dip chicken into Parmesan cheese first, then eggs, then panko. Heat oil in skillet. Brown chicken then place in baking dish. Pieces should not overlap. Place a slice of cheese on each breast.

Sauté mushrooms in butter or oil; add wine. Place mushrooms over chicken breasts and cover with liquid from pan. Bake 30 minutes (do not overcook or chicken will be dry). Garnish with chopped parsley and lemon juice or lemon wedges.

Mom's Award-Winning Ground Turkey/Veggie Chili

Submitted by Allen Akiona

My mom has never won a contest or hit it big in Las Vegas. But on the evening of the 80th Maui County fair, the stars aligned for my mom as she heard over the loud speakers, "The first place winner for *On Grandma's Table Contest* is Lois Akiona!" I wasn't back home on Maui to witness her proud moment, but my palate has always reminded me why the judges would vote for my mom's award-winning chili dish!

Serves 10 to 12

- 1 pound ground turkey
- 1 (1-inch) piece ginger, crushed
- 1/2 onion, diced
- 1 tablespoon cooking oil
- 1 teaspoon curry powder
- 2 teaspoons chili powder
- 2 (8-ounce) cans tomato sauce (no salt)
- 2 (10-3/4 ounce) cans condensed tomato soup (fat free)
- 2 stalks celery, sliced
- 2 carrots, sliced
- 2 zucchini, sliced
- 6 medium mushrooms, sliced
- 1 can kernel corn
- 1 can kidney beans
- 1 teaspoon Splenda, to taste

In a large pot, brown ground turkey, crushed ginger, and onion in oil until thoroughly cooked. Drain fat. Add curry powder and chili powder, mix well. Add remaining ingredients. Blend well and simmer on low heat for half an hour. Enjoy!

Note: Please keep in mind that this chili dish was originally made for diabetics and non-diabetics to enjoy.

Korean Turkey Patties

Submitted by Patricia Ann Tanaka

This recipe came from one of my sisters in Christ. She prepared this dish for us one day. What got my attention was when I noticed her two children, then ages ten and seven years old, really enjoying the turkey patties. I have adopted this recipe as a favorite. It's a healthier alternative to beef and you can often find a good deal on ground turkey at Costco!

Serves 4

1 pound ground turkey
3/4 cup raw oats (instant oatmeal)
1/4 cup Easy Korean Sauce (recipe follows)
1 egg

Easy Korean Sauce:
1/4 to 1/2 cup sugar
6 tablespoons shoyu
2 cloves mashed garlic
1 small smashed Hawaiian chili pepper
1 teaspoon sesame oil
1 teaspoon sesame seeds

Combine ingredients and shape into patties of any size. Fry in a skillet until light brown (don't overcook).

Mix Korean Sauce ingredients. Use as needed.

ʻŌpakapaka with Chinese Cabbage

Submitted by Jean Watanabe Hee

Out of all the recipes my mother passed on to me over the years, this dish is my favorite. Not only is it really delicious, it tastes and looks like it was prepared by a chef from a Chinese restaurant. My mother encouraged me to cook, and this was my first successful fish dish that everyone loved.

Serves 2 to 4

ʻŌpakapaka or mullet, cleaned
Salt and pepper to season
Flour for dredging
Oil for frying fish
1 stalk green onion, chopped

Gravy with Vegetables:
2 tablespoons chung choi (Chinese salted turnip), rinsed and chopped
4 shiitake mushrooms, soaked and sliced
1 small head Chinese cabbage, cut in 1-1/4 inch slices
1 piece garlic, crushed
1 piece ginger, crushed
1 teaspoon salt
1 teaspoon shoyu
1 teaspoon sugar
1-1/4 cups water
2 tablespoons cornstarch mixed with equal amount water

Sprinkle salt and pepper on fish. Coat with flour. Heat about 3 tablespoons oil and fry fish on medium heat. When fish is cooked, place onto serving platter and immediately sprinkle green onion over fish. In same frying pan used to cook fish, fry chung choi and mushrooms. Add Chinese cabbage and stir fry. When almost done, add garlic, ginger, seasonings, and water.

Thicken with cornstarch mixture. Pour Chinese cabbage and gravy over fried fish. Serve hot.

Seafood Curry

Submitted by Joanne V. Schergen

There's no better way to bringgenerationstogether than over a steaming bowl of seafood curry. While it isn't traditional "comfort food," it is a mixture of ingredients that comes together to create one fine dish.

Sort of like my family ... my mother, Virginia Schergen, adopted all five of her children from around the world. The eldest two are from Quebec, Canada, the middle child is from Italy, and the youngest two are from Chicago. When I was ten years old we moved to Hawai'i, making Pūpūkea our home. Growing up in Hawai'i, I was always finding so many interesting and delicious foods I wanted to learn how to cook.

My mother, a native mid-Westerner, did not stray too far from the foods that she was accustomed to. This meant that I was on my own. I remember going to the library and checking out local cookbooks. While I have never been too much of a daring eater—darn mid-Western roots—I did find a lot of local recipes that have helped me become more versatile in the kitchen. This recipe evolved over a few years as I experimented with a standard recipe I found as a teenager on the side of the Kingsford Baking Powder box. As I grew more daring in the kitchen, I started using coconut milk and tried different combinations of seafood.

Our growing family encompasses many cultures: Hawaiian, Filipino, Portuguese, Chinese, Japanese, and Caucasian. My seafood curry has been able to cross cultural borders to satisfy everyone's palate. A few of my children had been adamant curry-haters, but they now request this tasty dish for special occasions. It does a mother's heart good to be able to please her family and for me, this is one of those special dishes.

recipe continued on page 68

Serves 12

Sauce:
6 tablespoons yellow curry powder
6 tablespoons flour
6 tablespoons butter
1-1/2 cups milk
1-1/2 cups canned coconut milk
Salt, to taste

1/2 cup diced onion
1 tablespoon butter
Garlic salt, to taste
1/2 pound large scallops, connective tissue removed, cut in quarters
1 pound shrimp, peeled and deveined
1 piece sashimi-grade block 'ahi (or other fish, as desired), sliced 1/4-inch thick
8 ounces imitation crab pieces, cut in quarters
8 ounces frozen peas

To make sauce: Combine curry powder and flour. Melt butter in saucepan. Add curry and flour mixture, stirring 1 minute, until well mixed. Slowly whisk in both regular milk and coconut milk. Add salt and stir until sauce is boiling and thickened. Remove from heat. Cover with plastic wrap—let the plastic touch the surface, to keep a skin from forming.

Rinse seafood and dry on paper towel.

In a large skillet or dutch oven, sauté onions in butter. Add garlic salt. Once onions are translucent, add scallops, shrimp, and fish. Sauté, stirring occasionally until shrimp are pink and scallops are done. Add curry sauce, stirring gently.

Cut crab "legs" into quarters. Cook frozen peas as directed on bag. Add both to curry. Taste before serving and add more salt or garlic salt if needed. Simmer 5 minutes.

Serve with hot rice. May be garnished with mango chutney, fresh shredded coconut, and raisins.

Mom's Mahimahi Sauté Belle Meuniere

Submitted by Lolly Saari

My mom used to prepare this as a special meal on the weekends because during the week, she worked at my uncle's store in Pu'ukoli, and by the time she returned home, she couldn't prepare this dish in time for dinner. Because we had four children in our family, she had to prepare another entrée for my dad and two brothers, and we would enjoy a nice family meal together on Saturdays or Sundays.

Because the mahimahi was thick, I remember her slicing them on a slant to make thinner pieces.

Serves 4

8 (3-ounce) pieces mahimahi, thawed if frozen
1/4 cup milk
1/2 cup flour
1/2 teaspoon paprika
1 teaspoon salt
1/4 teaspoon ground white pepper
1/4 cup vegetable oil
1 teaspoon chopped parsley

Sauce:
1/2 to 3/4 stick butter
1 to 2 cloves garlic, minced
Juice from 1/2 lemon

Lemon slices (garnish)

Remove skin from fish. Cut into pieces by slicing on a slant to create thinner slices. Place in bowl with milk. Combine flour, paprika, salt and pepper. Remove fish from milk and dredge in flour mixture.

Heat oil in skillet; brown fish fillets and place on serving platter. Sprinkle with more paprika and parsley.

To make sauce: Melt butter in skillet. Add garlic. Add lemon juice. Cook until garlic is lightly browned. Pour sauce over fish; garnish with lemons slices.

Pan-Fried Moana with Asian-Style Remoulade

Submitted by Brooke Tadena

My dad, Herman's, passion was to dive. He'd go out every chance to be in the ocean and thankfully he was rewarded with many treasures. As long as I can remember, his best friends were the commercial fishermen. They would be at our house to fry ono, smoke 'ahi, or steam their "catch of the day." My dad dived, but he had a fisherman's mentality. They utilized every part of their catch. We had aku belly, fish head soups.

Subsequently savoring a wide range of tasty backyard cooking, my siblings and I learned from eating various concoctions of flavors.

I yearned to expand my eating horizons. Attending culinary school developed a deeper sense of appreciation of subtle flavors we have to offer in the Islands. Now I prepare the tastiest pizzas and hamburgers for my three princesses.

Serves 6

6 locally caught moana, scaled, cleaned, gutted (1 per person)
Salt
Ground white pepper
1 cup all-purpose flour
Vegetable oil for frying

Asian Remoulade:
1 cup Best Foods mayonnaise
1 tablespoon fine chopped takuan
1 tablespoon pickled cucumber
1 tablespoon finely chopped Cilantro
1 tablespoon finely sliced green onion
1 tablespoon Yamasa shoyu

Season the moana with salt and pepper. Dredge in flour and shake off the excess. Pan-fry in vegetable oil at medium-high heat on both sides until fish is crisp and nicely caramelized.

Add all the ingredients for the remoulade to a mixing bowl and mix well.

Note: The fish could be substituted with any local or seasonal fish. This could be served as an appetizer, with salad greens, or as an enhancement to a entrée.

Gambas with Spanish Sauce

Submitted by Jovita R. Zimmerman

Gambas is a Spanish dish we normally serve for festive meals during the "Noche Buena," after attending midnight mass, for a special birthday, or other important family anniversary. I'd describe this dish as important as a relleno dish, or lechon, or grilled pork.

Serves 4

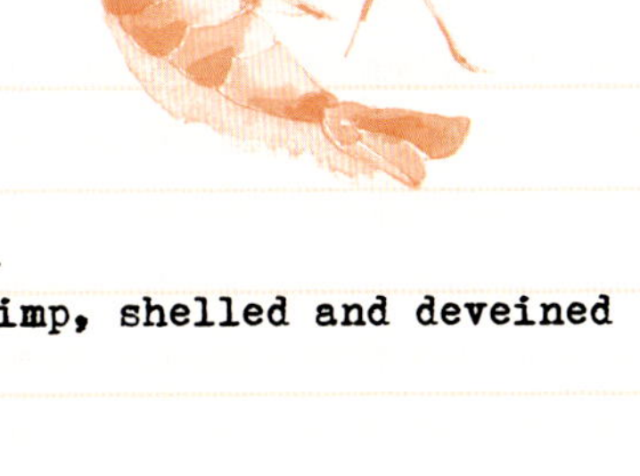

Spanish Tomato Sauce:
1 clove garlic, crushed
1/2 cup onion, chopped fine
1/4 cup olive oil
1 cup tomato sauce

5 cloves garlic, minced
1/4 cup olive or vegetable oil
2-1/4 pounds medium-sized shrimp, shelled and deveined
1 teaspoon lemon juice
1/2 cup white wine
Dash of hot chili sauce
1 to 2 tablespoons bread crumbs, optional
Black olives, for garnish

To make sauce: Sauté garlic and onion in olive oil. Add tomato sauce. Simmer gently for 30 to 60 minutes.

Brown garlic in olive oil. Add shrimp; toss until pink. Add lemon juice, wine, chili sauce, and 2 tablespoons Spanish Tomato Sauce. Cook 1 minute more. Thicken with bread crumbs, if necessary. Serve on a mound of rice, garnish with olives.

Ratatouille

Submitted by Julie Robley

While on a visit to Hawai'i, my Aunty Demy surprised us all by cooking (she is not one to cook) and made this fabulously tasty vegetable dish. My mother and I instantly fell in love with it but Aunty refused to share the recipe, claiming that her dear friend—a chef in one of the best Italian restaurants in Monterey, Calif.—taught it to her on the condition that she not share the recipe with anyone.

The next day, Mommy heated up the leftovers for lunch. I noticed her "picking" at the food— she was trying to figure out what was in it. I joined in and we came up with most of the ingredients. Over the next week, we tried and tried and came about as close as we could to what Aunty had made. When we served it to Aunty, the look on her face was simply priceless! "How in the world did you do this?" she said.

After dinner, Mommy and Aunty talked about the ingredients and preparation. The only thing we were missing was olive oil, which made all the difference in the taste. The next day, we trekked off to the store to purchase the ingredients and made the dish again. This time it was a complete success.

When I make this dish, I find myself giggling and remembering all that we went through to get this recipe, and I will forever remember the look on Aunty's face and the laughter we all shared!

recipe continued on page 74

Serves 4

1/3 cup olive oil
2 onions, halved then sliced
2 cloves garlic, mashed
2 green peppers, sliced
2 to 3 long eggplant, sliced
2 zucchini, sliced
1 large tomato, diced OR 1 (28-ounce) can diced tomatoes
1/2 cup cilantro
1 bay leaf
1 teaspoon oregano leaves
1 teaspoon basil
2 teaspoons salt, or to taste
1 teaspoon ground pepper

Heat oil in pot. Add onion, garlic, and green peppers. Sauté 10 minutes.

Add eggplant and zucchini. Mix gently. Cover and simmer 20 minutes.

Add tomato, cilantro, bay leaf, oregano, basil, salt and pepper. Cover and simmer 20 minutes. Serve hot or cold.

Cheese Nut Patties

Submitted by Melanie Kohler

I threw together this recipe many years ago when my sons were young and I was trying to cut back on eating meat—both for health and cost-cutting reasons. It has become one of my family's favorites, even though we are not vegetarians. It's a very versatile recipe and can easily be adjusted to your own family's tastes.

I find it extra helpful to make up a huge batch when I have time and freeze the patties so they are on hand for quick family meals. This does not always happen, though, because when the extended family hears that I've made some cheese nut patties, the requests start rolling in. Before I know it, my "huge batch" has all been given away in one-dozen packages, and it's time to make more!

Makes 2 to 3 dozen (3-inch diameter) patties. If making patties large enough for burgers, yield is 18 to 24.

1 onion, chopped fine
3 cups brown rice, cooked
2 cups shredded cheddar cheese
1 cup walnuts, chopped
1/2 cup bread crumbs
1/2 teaspoon dried parsley flakes, optional
4 eggs, beaten
Salt and pepper, to taste
Vegetable oil, for frying

Combine onion, rice, cheese, nuts, bread crumbs, and parsley. (A food processor can be used to chop onion and walnuts, shred cheese and make bread crumbs.) Add eggs, salt and pepper; mix well. Form into patties about 3 inches in diameter.

Heat oil in skillet and fry patties until golden.

Serve with rice or in a hamburger bun, or to make it as a casserole, place fried patties in a casserole dish, cover with marinara sauce or cream of mushroom soup, and bake for 10 to 15 minutes at 350°F until hot and bubbly.

Old-Time Okinawan Pancakes

Submitted by Helen Azama Furuya

This simple pancake was taught to my dad by his mother, Ushiya Azama (1890–1984). It was one giant breakfast pancake. Growing up, Dad would prepare it for us when Mom was gone two to three hours visiting with her mother who lived two doors down from us. This recipe is special because it came from Grandma and because Dad, who Mom always said "doesn't know how to cook," made it for us five kids. Can you image Mom's disbelief when I asked him for the recipe over thirty years ago?

My father, Richard Azama, circa 1930 standing on Kaneohe farm.

Makes 8 wedges

- 2 cups unsifted flour
- 2 heaping teaspoons baking powder
- 1/2 cup sugar
- 2 large eggs
- 1 cup water
- 1/4 cup vegetable oil (for 9-inch cast-iron frying pan)
- Butter, jam or jelly for filling

Measure and mix dry ingredients. Set aside. Add beaten eggs to water. Set aside.

Heat 1/4 cup oil in frying pan on medium heat. Tilt the pan around to coat oil about halfway up on all sides of pan. Combine liquid with the dry ingredients and stir to blend well but do not over mix. Pour batter into heated pan and cover (leaving a small vent). Turn heat to low right away. Keep covered 18 to 20 minutes. Remove cover, loosen sides and underside with a spatula and gently flip. Cook top-side down for another 2 to 4 minutes and test for doneness with a toothpick. Turn onto serving platter. Use a paper towel to absorb any excess oil and cut into 8 wedges. Slit across center of wedge, slather on butter and your favorite jam or jelly. Other kinds of filling are fine, too. Sometimes Dad put in a piece of fried bacon. This pancake is great eaten hot!

Nancy Azama Takata and Ushiya Azama in front of fruit and vegetable stand on Kamehameha Highway.

Salads, Soups, and Stews

These refreshing recipes are sophisticated offerings that can stand on their own. There's a smoked salmon salad that includes Japanese soba and wakame. Maui Onion and orange salad is dressed with the lively flavors of Dijon mustard and lemon, plus more. A Thai selection seasons jasmine rice with yellow curry and a touch of fish sauce and combines it with a host of fresh vegetables.

You'll also find the kind of comfort foods that soothe the soul on a rainy day or sate a hearty appetite after a long day at the beach. These are favorite family stew recipes, both familiar and unique, plus soups with ethnic flair. Within this chapter, see also a special section dedicated to Portuguese bean soup, which can be prepared in a variety of ways with an array of ingredients.

Maui Onion and Orange Salad

Submitted by Julie Robley

Mommy got this recipe from her godfather, Alfred Marteles, on Maui sometime in the mid-1980s. She thought this was a "haute" dish as it included "good expensive stuff": Dijon mustard. At that time, cooking was very "black and white," and combining two ingredients such as onions and oranges was unheard of. But it was so yummy and Uncle was overjoyed to share this dish with us. The only problem was that there were no measurements, so we had to go home and make it repeatedly until we could figure it all out. Yup, Listerine made a bunch of money off us in the next couple of months!

Serves 4

5 navel oranges, peeled
1 large Maui onion, thinly sliced and separated into rings
Zest of 1 lemon
3 tablespoons lemon juice
1 teaspoon Dijon mustard
1/4 cup olive oil
3 tablespoons orange juice
1/2 teaspoon salt
1/4 teaspoon pepper
1 bunch watercress, stems removed
1/3 cup minced fresh mint leaves (optional)

Peel oranges, removing all white membrane. Slice crosswise into round pieces, reserving as much as of the juice as possible. Place slices and juice in a serving bowl. Add onion rings and sprinkle with lemon zest.

In a separate bowl, whisk together lemon juice, mustard, olive oil, orange juice, salt and pepper. Pour over orange mixture, toss and refrigerate until serving.

To serve: Tuck watercress around edges of serving bowl and sprinkle with mint, if desired.

Smoked Salmon Soba Salad

Submitted by Mary Lou Toyama

Dad and Mom Masue grew green onions and daikon in Koko Head, what is now Mariner's Cove, and sold them at open markets. These two vegetables were always plentiful in our household.

Growing is in our blood. Our family has been in Kamilonui Valley for over 40 years growing everything from watermelons to dwarf apple bananas. We take the practice of farm-to-table seriously. Every week, my sister Kathy and I sell our bananas at the People's Open Market, and my brother, Jerry, plants and harvests.

All the ingredients in this dish create a healthy dish. It's a meal in itself. Sometimes I use yamaimo potato noodles, which are firmer and taste better, instead of buckwheat noodles.

This is a contagious dish. Once you try this recipe, it may become your potluck contribution. Everyone who shares this dish at a special gathering is always asked for the recipe.

Whenever I make this dish or use daikon or green onion, I think of my dad. He told me the true purpose of fresh daikon was to help aid in the digestion of seafood.

recipe continued on page 84

Serves 10

1/3 cup dry wakame
1 (10-ounce) package soba noodles
1 (6-inch-long) dashi konbu, cut into 4 pieces
1 red round onion, thinly sliced
1 Japanese cucumber, thinly sliced
14 ounces ocean salad
1 pound smoked salmon
1 daikon, thinly sliced
1 carrot, thinly sliced
1 red bell pepper, sliced horizontally and thinly
3 stalks green onion, thinly sliced

Dressing:
1/3 cup sugar
1 tablespoon sesame oil
1 teaspoon black pepper
2 tablespoons sake
1-1/2 teaspoons salt
2 tablespoons fresh lemon juice
1/3 cup Japanese vinegar
1/2 cup vegetable oil

Soak wakame in water for 1 hour, then wash, drain and cut into small pieces.

Meanwhile, make dressing: Combine all ingredients and mix well. Set aside.

In boiling water, add soba noodles and dashi konbu. Cook soba according to package directions. Drain well. Place noodles in a 9x13-inch pan.

Layer with red onion, wakame, cucumbers, ocean salad, salmon, daikon, carrots, red pepper, and green onion. Drizzle with dressing.

Thai Yellow Curry Rice Salad

Submitted by Audrey Wilson

I first visited Thailand in 2003 and fell in love with the country, the people and the food! Every year after that, my husband, Jim, and I visited Lampang, Thailand, to teach English to elementary and high school students there. I created this salad because of my love for their foods. I love this salad for buffets because it is not only colorful, but delicious. The yellow curries and turmeric mixed with the rice give it a vivid yellow color that pops along side the colorful carrots, peas, and red and green bell peppers. It is my version of "fried rice," only healthier. I use fish sauce instead of shoyu to season the rice, and instead of frozen peas, you can add shelled edamame or soybeans.

Serves 4 to 6

- 1 cup uncooked jasmine rice
- 1 tablespoon canola oil
- 1 teaspoon Thai yellow curry paste
- 1 teaspoon sweet curry powder
- 1/4 teaspoon ground turmeric
- 2 tablespoons shredded carrots
- 1/2 cup frozen peas, boiled in water for 5 minutes, then drained
- 1/2 teaspoon Thai fish sauce (nam pla)
- 1/2 cup raisins
- 1/2 cup chopped, seeded tomatoes
- 1/2 cup green and red sweet bell peppers, diced into 1/8-inch pieces
- 2 tablespoons chopped green onions
- 2 tablespoons chopped cilantro
- 2 tablespoons chopped peanuts or cashews

Wash jasmine rice, drain, add 1 cup water, cook rice for 20 minutes until all the water is gone and rice is cooked. Place oil in pan. When hot, add curries and turmeric. Cook till fragrant. While rice is still hot, add the oil, curries and turmeric mixture to rice. Add shredded carrots, peas, and season with fish sauce. Add raisins, tomatoes, and bell peppers, and mix well. Place rice salad on platter and scatter with chopped onions, cilantro, and chopped nuts.

Portuguese White Bean Soup

Submitted by John Serrao

My father cooked this soup frequently during World War II due to food rations. The recipe can be expanded for larger families and lasts several days. After three generations, this soup is still a family favorite because it doesn't use too many ingredients, is easy to cook and tastes great.

Serves 8

1 package small white beans
Water
2 medium potatoes
1 pound Oscar Mayer bacon, cut into 1-inch pieces
Salt, to taste
2 bunches watercress, washed and cut into 2-inch lengths

Rinse white beans and place in stock pot. Fill halfway with water. Soak beans overnight.

When ready to begin cooking, pour out the water and rinse beans. Refill the pot 3/4 full with water. Cook on medium heat until tender.

Stir occasionally so beans do not stick to the bottom of the pot. Add potatoes and bacon. Stir gently.

When potatoes are cooked, turn off heat. Add salt to taste and watercress. Press watercress gently into the broth. Do not mix until ready to serve. Goes great with warm bread.

Portuguese Bean and Vegetable Soup

Submitted by Eleanora Cadinha

This is a hearty recipe passed on from my mom to me, with some of my own touches. My family and neighbors enjoy this recipe, and it is a favorite request for Super Bowl parties and fundraisers. I have a wonderful neighbor, Steve, and whenever I make it I call him and ask if he'd like a pot. He always responds, "Is the Pope Catholic?" and rushes right over with his pot in hand.

Serves 12 to 15

Portuguese Spice:

2 bottles whole anise
1 bottle stick cinnamon
1 bottle whole cloves
1 bottle peppercorns

1 pound dried kidney beans
3 large ham shanks
6 cups water
2 Portuguese sausages, cut into bite-size pieces
2 large, meaty soup bones, with any meat cut into bite-size pieces
1 tablespoon Hawaiian salt
1 teaspoon pepper
1 large onion, diced
1 large half-ripe papaya, diced
2 (8-ounce) cans tomato sauce
1/4 cup cider vinegar
1 pound carrots, cubed
4 stalks celery, cut into 1/4-inch pieces
4 large russet potatoes, cubed
1 medium cabbage, chopped
1 bunch watercress, cut into 1/4-inch pieces
2 bay leaves
1 teaspoon Portuguese spice

To make Portuguese spice, put all spices in a large baking pan and toast at 350°F until crisp, about 30 minutes.

Place in a plastic bag and smash into bits, then run through a coffee or spice grinder and grind until fine. Store in jars.

For soup, soak beans overnight. Rinse beans.

In pot, combine beans, ham, and water, cover then simmer for 1 hour, or until beans are tender. Let cool (save liquid from beans). Remove bones, skim off fat and cut meat into bite-size pieces.

In a large pot, brown sausage, beef, and soup bones. Add half of the salt and pepper, onions and papaya, and sauté lightly. Stir in tomato sauce and vinegar and cook for 5 minutes.

Add 2 cups water and simmer 1 hour. Add carrots and celery and cook an additional 20 minutes. Add potatoes and cook another 20 minutes.

Add cabbage, watercress, ham, and reserved liquid, plus Portuguese spice, bay leaf, and the rest of the salt and pepper. Cook until vegetables are tender and soup is thick.

Portuguese Bean Soup with Lentils and Butternut Squash

Submitted by James Ahia

My wife and I adapted this version of Portuguese bean soup after trying many recipes, and I feel it is finely tuned. It has become a much-requested potluck dish. I believe in willingly sharing the joys I get from cooking, so do what you want with it. This soup is great to make when you have at least 4 or 5 hours to spare, company is expected, and it is raining. We baked some old-fashioned Pa'o Doce to go with the soup.

Serves 8

- 2 smoked ham hocks (1-1/2 to 2 pounds)
- 1 small kabocha (ujiki and butternut OK, too)
- 1 to 2 (10- to 12-ounce) Portuguese sausages (linguisa or kielbasa are OK, too)
- 1 medium round onion, chopped
- 2 cans pinto beans (or kidney, if preferred)
- 1 can Progresso lentil soup
- 1/4 cup ketchup
- 3 tablespoons dark brown sugar
- 1 tablespoon minced dried parsley
- 6 dried bay leaves
- 1 cup small macaroni noodles
- Fresh watercress, cut into 1-inch lengths (optional)

Place ham hocks and onions in a large, deep pot with water to cover. Bring to a boil, then lower heat to simmer until meat softens and starts to fall off bones.

While hocks are simmering, clean, peel and cut squash into 1-inch cubes. Set aside.

When hocks are soft, remove bones, cut meat into small pieces and return to pot. Slice sausage in half lengthwise, then in 1/4-inch pieces, and add to pot. Add squash.

recipe continued on page 92

Add the rest of the ingredients except macaroni and watercress, if using.

Continue cooking until squash is easy to cut with a stirring spoon. Add macaroni and simmer until noodles are soft. Adjust seasoning if necessary.

If using, add watercress about 10 minutes before serving.

My Family's Portuguese Bean Soup

Submitted by Florence Cabrera

Though there are many varieties of Portuguese bean soup, this one is special to me because it came from my mom. She must have learned it from my father, since she was Hawaiian and he immigrated from Puerto Rico to Hawai'i. I've been cooking it since I was 16 years old. When I worked at the Crouching Lion, locals and mainlanders alike complimented me on this soup. I've made changes over the years to suit my taste. Now, I mostly make the soup for holidays, birthdays, and other family get-togethers.

Serves 8

2 ham shanks
4 medium potatoes cut in cubes
6 cloves garlic, minced
1 bunch cilantro, chopped
1 medium onion, chopped
2 (8-ounce) cans tomato sauce
1 (15-ounce) can kidney beans
4 ounces spaghetti noodles
Salt, to taste
2 cups cut watercress, cut in 1-inch pieces

Boil ham shanks until soft. Add water as needed.

Add all the vegetables except watercress. Add tomato sauce and kidney beans. Cook until the vegetables are almost done, then add noodles and simmer until cooked. Add the watercress. Cook for 3 minutes. Serve with garlic toast.

Mom's Portuguese Bean Soup

Submitted by Pua Mei

This was my mom's recipe. Back in the day of gala legislature openings, my sister-in-law made huge pots of this soup, and the celebrants would line the halls waiting for a cup. Truly 'ono!

Serves 8 to 10

- 1 pound small red beans
- 3 pounds ham hocks
- 5 to 6 cloves garlic, minced
- Freshly ground pepper
- 5 to 6 tablespoons Worcestershire sauce
- 2 large Maui onions, diced
- 4 large potatoes, cubed
- 4 large carrots, diced
- 2 spicy Portuguese sausages
- 1 (8-ounce) can tomato sauce
- 1 small cabbage, shredded
- 1 tablespoon Hawaiian sea salt

Soak beans overnight. Drain and rinse.

Place beans in a large soup pot and cover with water (or chicken stock). Add all other ingredients except cabbage and salt. Bring to a boil. Simmer 3 hours or longer. Add extra liquid if necessary.

Remove ham hocks, remove the bones, skin and fat, break up meat and return to pot. Add cabbage and salt. Test for seasoning and adjust accordingly.

Simmer an additional 30 minutes. Serve with buttered Portuguese sweet bread.

Rose Freitas's Portuguese Bean Soup

Submitted by Laureen Freitas

This recipe was taught to my grandmother, Mary Ferreira, who later taught it to my mom, Rosaline Freitas. My mother would cook this on cold, rainy days or whenever someone requested it. I would take a big pot of this soup to work for potlucks at Kapi'olani Medical Center, where I worked as a nurse for many years. Nurses, doctors, supervisory staff—everyone just waited for Laureen's mom's soup!

Serves 8 to 10

1 (16-ounce) package pink pinto beans
3 to 4 medium frozen ham hocks, or ham shank
1 large white onion, chopped
1 Portuguese sausage, chopped
2 (8-ounce) cans tomato sauce
4 potatoes, chopped
1 carrot, chopped
4 garlic cloves, crushed
1/2 box of macaroni
Salt, pepper and garlic salt, to taste
1 bunch watercress, top through mid-stem, chopped

Rinse dried beans. Place in a large pot with ham hocks and onions, then add enough water to fill 3/4 of the pot. Boil 3 to 4 hours.

Add sausage, tomato sauce, potatoes, carrots, and garlic. Debone ham hocks, then return meat to pot. Add salt, garlic salt, and pepper to taste and cook another 30 to 45 minutes.

Turn off stove and add macaroni and watercress. Eat with French bread.

Oxtail Soup

Submitted by Carol Chun

I'm Japanese, but I was married to a great Chinese cook. He learned to cook from his mother, and I learned to cook Chinese food from watching him, his mother, and his great aunt. Nothing was ever written down and you eventually learned to improvise. This final version of oxtail soup came after many good and bad attempts. I like vegetables in my soup so I added the daikon and carrots. It's a time-consuming process but worth it. I won an oxtail soup showdown at Punahou School last year. The judges said my version made them think of the oxtail soup they ate when they were growing up. I hope that my children will enjoy this soup for many years to come. Long, slow cooking is like life itself: a long, evolving process.

Serves 4

- 1 tray oxtail
- 2 tablespoons oil
- 2 inches fresh ginger, skinned and cut in half
- 1 can chicken broth and 1 can water
- 1 chung choi (salted turnip bundle, available in Asian food markets)
- 1 daikon, about 6 inches long, peeled and cut into half-moon shape
- 1 large carrot, peeled and cut in chunks
- 1 package (12 ounces) shiitake mushrooms, soaked and cut in half with stems removed
- 1 package blanched peanuts
- Cilantro (optional), for garnish
- Grated ginger, for dipping

Brown oxtails in oil in a large soup pot. Cover with water. Add ginger. Bring to a boil to clean tails, then drain and rinse.

Using the same pot, put in oxtails, ginger chunks, chicken broth and water (add more water if necessary, to cover oxtails.) Add chung choi. Bring to a boil, then simmer until oxtails are tender to the touch.

Put liquid in a separate container and refrigerate oxtails and broth overnight. Fat will rise to the top and harden; scrape off hardened fat and discard.

Put 1/3 of the broth (it should look gelatinous) in pot with oxtails and heat on low.

Put the remaining broth and daikon, carrots and mushrooms in a separate pot and bring to a boil, then simmer until veggies are fork-tender.

Add peanuts after 30 minutes—watch your liquid levels. Combine both pots and taste broth to adjust water if it's too salty, then serve.

Rainy Day Soup

Submitted by Alben Aduca

This soup was created by my late mother for cold, rainy days. It was also perfect after a long day of surfing, or when I was feeling sick. Not only did I enjoy it, but I think my dad did, too—I would often see this in his "kau kau tin." This soup doesn't take long to make, maybe 15 minutes, yet it is a flavorful recipe, very light. It goes well with rice in the bowl.

Serves 2 to 3

- **1 (15-ounce) can salmon or diced fresh salmon**
- **1 (15-ounce) can chicken broth**
- **1 or 2 cloves garlic, crushed**
- **1/2 onion, thinly sliced**
- **4 shiitake mushrooms, soaked and thinly sliced (optional)**
- **1 tablespoon patis (fish sauce, optional)**
- **1 package long rice (glass noodle, bean thread, or vermicelli noodle)**
- **1 stalk green onion, cut into 1-inch pieces**

Cook all the ingredients in a small pot over medium heat for about 10 minutes, adding the long rice noodle and green onion last. Simmer for about 3 to 5 minutes and serve hot.

Note: The noodles will absorb the broth, so add more broth if desired.

Kaūmana-Style Scallop Soup

Submitted by Sandy Uemura

My family and I reside in Kaūmana, a suburb of Hilo on Hawaiʻi Island. Because of the cold climate, I've included soup as part of my family's meals. One cold winter morning while in bed, I began to think "soups" and came up with this recipe. It has been a favorite among family and friends for quite a few years. My children are adults now, and they still love soup whether it's warm or cold. Hopefully, the soup recipes that I have created will be passed on by my children to their own families.

Serves 6 to 7

7 to 8 cups water
6 to 8 dried shrimp
1 can (14.5-ounce) chicken broth
1 to 2 tablespoons cornstarch
4 shiitake mushrooms, soaked in warm water for 15 minutes and sliced 1/4-inch thick
7 fresh oyster mushrooms, sliced 1/4-inch thick
Salt, to taste
1 small package Nice brand long rice, soaked in warm water for 15 minutes, then drained and cut into 2-inch pieces
1 tray frozen small scallops
2 eggs, beaten
3 to 4 stalks green onions, cut into 1/4-inch pieces (garnish)

On medium heat in a pot, combine water and shrimp. Boil for 30 minutes. Add chicken broth and continue boiling.

Remove one cup of the soup and cool. When cooled, combine with cornstarch. Mix until smooth. Set aside.

Add the mushrooms to the soup. Add salt to taste.

Gradually add cornstarch mixture to the soup. Stir until soup is slightly thick.

Add long rice and continue cooking until noodles are opaque. Add scallops and cook for 3 minutes. In a bowl, beat the eggs, then with a fork, stir eggs into the pot.

Immediately remove from heat. Garnish with green onions.

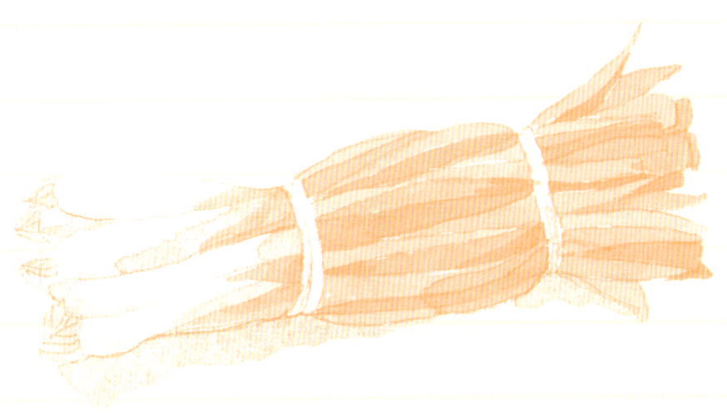

Chicken Rice Soup

Submitted by Florence Cabrera

I made up this recipe one day when I had a lot of leftover chicken. My family loved it, so I started making it for special family occasions because it's fast, easy, and very tasty. This soup works with any kind of chicken—uncooked or cooked leftovers. I sometimes chop or shred rotisserie chicken from Costco. No matter what kind you decide to use, the soup will be ʻono.

Serves 6

3 cups cooked chicken
1 medium onion, chopped
1 bunch cilantro, chopped
1 small can mushrooms, drained
1/4 cup raw rice, rinsed, or handful spaghetti noodles
3 cans chicken broth
Salt, to taste
Spaghetti noodles (optional)

In a medium stock pot add chicken, vegetables, mushrooms and rice or noodles. Add chicken broth, salt, and noodles, if using.

Cook on medium heat for about 30 minutes if using rice, or about 15 minutes if using noodles.

Green Papaya and Chicken Soup

Submitted by Colleen Roberts-Witt

My mother and her older sisters cooked this simple but tasty soup while living at 9-1/2 Mile Camp (mile post 9-1/2), better known as ʻŌlaʻa Plantation, on the island of Hawaiʻi. Sometimes Mom would add a dash of Aloha Shoyu for color. She said that her family's daily meals on the plantation usually consisted of Mānoa lettuce dipped in shoyu with hot rice, so you can imagine what a treat it was to have this hot, delicious soup instead. It's a real comfort food for me, and I made it for my children when they were growing up, and for my grandchildren, too.

Serves 6

- 6 chicken thighs, with or without bone
- 2 large garlic cloves, chopped
- 1/2 onion, chopped
- 1/2 teaspoon salt
- 3 large green papayas, chopped into large chunks (papaya should be totally green)
- Salt and pepper, to taste
- 1 tablespoon Aloha Shoyu, to taste (optional)
- Pinch cayenne (optional)

Boil about 10 cups of water in a large soup pot. Add chicken thighs, garlic, onion, and salt.

Boil 10 minutes, then add green papaya to the pot. Simmer 45 minutes until papaya is tender. Add pepper and more salt if necessary.

Add shoyu and cayenne if using. Serve with rice, quinoa, or just by itself.

Simple Crock Pot Jook

Submitted by Steve Dung

I can remember always having to wait for Thanksgiving or some special event where turkey was served before my mom would make jook. Well, now I don't have to wait.

I love my crock pot! It's a trouble-free way to keep my family nourished and happy. We all have busy lives. It's a gift of balance to keep all the balls in the air at the same time.

I have a busy life working my day job then picking up Erin, my daughter, from school. Between soccer practice and piano, we barely have time to sit together for a family dinner, let alone shopping and preparing meals.

In the evening, after dinner, I fill my little crock pot with all the ingredients for the jook. The hard part—shopping for all the ingredients—is done earlier. Sun Chong Grocery has everything. All we do is call in our order, and when they see us pull into their drive way, they wheel out our groceries to our car!

Turn the crock pot on low for eight hours and wake up to the rich aroma of ham and rice gruel.

Serves 4

2 smoked ham hocks (see note)
5 quarts water
1-1/2 cups white rice
6 to 8 pieces dried mushrooms
1/2 cup raw peanuts
2 slivers ginger (optional)
Dried bean curd (optional)

Put ham hocks in the crock pot, fill with water, add rice, mushrooms, peanuts, ginger, and bean curd. Switch the crock pot on low for 8 hours. The crock pot can stay on for up to 10 hours. Can be started before you go to bed and you'll wake up to the aroma of fresh jook for breakfast.

Note: Smoked ham hocks can be substituted with smoked turkey or turkey bones.

Maui-Style Hawaiian Stew

Submitted by Clarence Kawana

This was a popular family gathering dish of Ed Hirai, who passed away in February. He was born in Pā'ia, Maui, and was a longtime resident of Kula. Approximately one year before his passing, Ed said he learned this recipe from his mother, Miyuki Hirai of Pā'ia Store. This is a recipe appropriate for beginner cooks. In fact, Ed's famous words were "this soup is so easy to prepare." At his memorial service on February 14, 2011, 60 copies of Ed's handwritten recipes were distributed.

Serves 6 to 8

1-1/2 pounds stew meat
2 tablespoons oil
7 cloves garlic, minced
2 or 3 celery stalks, sliced
2 large carrots, sliced
4 large ripe tomatoes, chopped
Salt, to taste
2 Irish potatoes, sliced in chunks
1 sweet round onion, sliced
1 can tomato sauce
String beans or cabbage (optional)

In a big pot, fry stew meat in 2 tablespoons oil, until brown. Add water and boil for 20 to 30 minutes. Drain water and add new water, and boil again.

After water starts to boil, see if the water stays clean. If so, add garlic, celery, carrots, and chopped tomatoes. Let it boil for hours until stew becomes orange.

Add salt and potato chunks with sliced round onions and tomato sauce. Boil on low heat until done.

Grams's ʻOno Oxtail Stew

Submitted by Leina Awai

Grams is the best cook ever! We love her stews, all kinds of stews from lūʻau and beef to curry and especially oxtail. Yep, we said oxtail. We live in Kula where we ranch and rodeo. Grams's oxtail stew has been a family tradition for years. We'd get the oxtail straight from DeCoite's Packing House and Grams would get it home and straight into the pot. I think most of Maui knows about it because people would talk about how Grams would make it at our rodeos and parties. They couldn't get enough of it, and now neither can we!

Serves 4

2-1/2 pounds oxtail, cut at joints
1 large Kula onion, coarsely chopped
1 large stalk celery, cut into 1-inch pieces
1 (12-ounce) can tomato paste
1/2 teaspoon black pepper
2 teaspoons Hawaiian salt
1 teaspoon oregano
3 large garlic cloves
1 teaspoon sugar
2 large potatoes, cut into large cubes
2 carrots, cut into 2-inch pieces

Place oxtail in large pot and add water to cover tails. Add all ingredients except potatoes and carrots. Boil 3 to 3-1/2 hours adding more water as needed until just tender. Stir frequently to prevent from burning. Add potatoes and carrots and cook until vegetables are done. Serve over rice or with poi and/or pineapple coleslaw. If you refrigerate for later, skim off excess oil before warming.

Chinese Chicken Stew

Submitted by Donna Kelsey

I was living on another island, and when I would return home to visit, my mother would always cook wonderful meals for me. Growing up, she prepared Chinese chicken stew for family dinners, and I loved it but took it for granted. I had not thought about it for a long time, but when she prepared it on one of my visits home, it tasted especially good because she had made it just for me. It brought back a flood of warm memories of us in the kitchen together, as well as some of the other delicious meals she had prepared.

Makes 12 to 16 cups

7 to 9 pieces boneless, skinless chicken thighs (about 2 to 3 pounds)
1 (14.5-ounce) can low-sodium chicken broth and enough water to just cover the chicken
1 (8-ounce) can whole water chestnuts, drained, rinsed in cold water and sliced in half
1 (15-ounce) can whole bamboo shoots, drained, rinsed in cold water and sliced in half lengthwise, then in 1/2-inch slices
1 (7-ounce) bag of dried bean curd sticks (Break into 1-2 pieces, soak in a bowl of warm water to soften. Find this in the Oriental section of your supermarket or in Chinatown.)
7 to 9 whole pieces of aburage, cut into 1-inch slices
1 large round onion, cut into 1/2-inch squares
1 inch fresh ginger, grated
3 pieces fresh ginger, cut into 1/2-inch slices and crushed with handle of a big knife
1 heaping teaspoon finely minced garlic
1/2 teaspoon ground white pepper, or to taste
1 to 2 teaspoons kosher or Hawaiian salt (optional)
1 small package dried black fungus, rinsed and soaked in warm water, then squeezed to remove excess water
1/2 to 3/4 cup barley, rinsed
8 whole black Chinese or shiitake mushrooms, soaked in warm water to soften, then rinsed and squeezed to remove excess water
5 to 7 pieces whole Chinese five-star anise
1 teaspoon sugar or agave

Thickener:

2 to 3 tablespoons cornstarch
3 to 4 tablespoons water
1 teaspoon shoyu

Garnish:

1 cup green onions, cut into 1- to 2-inch lengths
1 bunch cilantro, cut into 1- to 2-inch lengths

Put all the ingredients in a large pot and bring to a boil.

Or, if you have a pressure cooker, put all the ingredients in it and cook on high for 30 minutes. Make sure the cooker has room to spare; a 16-cup cooker should work fine.

This is not a very salty dish. Adjust the salt and sugar until it tastes just right for you.

Add the thickener slowly, stirring constantly. This should be a hearty, thick stew. When thickened to desired consistency, bring the stew to a boil to cook the cornstarch thoroughly, then turn off heat and remove from the burner.

Garnish with green onions and cilantro. Stir garnish into the stew when you are ready to serve.

Lūʻau Stew

Submitted by Ernie Bautista and Roxanne Tunoa

This recipe came from my mom through our Hawaiian tūtū. My mom grew up in a small house way back in Pauoa Valley, on the corner of Booth Road. Back then, Pauoa Valley used a lot of the water resources that came from the surrounding mountains, so residents were able to maintain rice paddies and taro patches. Because of the large availability of taro leaves and the economical price of beef brisket, my tūtū was able to make a big pot of lūʻau stew for her very large family of ten. Then, when I was a child visiting tūtū on Sundays, tūtū would still make a big pot of lūʻau stew to kaukau. Brings back many fond memories of my tūtū and visiting her back in Pauoa Valley.

Serves 8

2 pounds lūʻau leaves
4 pounds beef brisket
2 tablespoons vegetable oil
2 cloves garlic
3 cans beef broth
5 cups water
1 tablespoon Hawaiian salt

recipe continued on page 110

Clean lūʻau leaves and save stems. Cut brisket into 2-inch pieces.

Heat oil in large, heavy pot and place in brisket with garlic cloves. Be sure garlic does not burn. When meat is brown, add broth, water, and salt.

Simmer for 3 hours. Check liquid in the pot periodically. It should cover the beef. Add water as necessary.

When beef is tender add lūʻau leaves and simmer another 1-1/2 hours. Be sure that the leaves are well cooked. (A lot of shrinkage will occur with the leaves.)

Serve with rice or poi.

Portuguese Stew

Submitted by Bernadette Rapozo-Mattos

This is a cherished dish from my mom, Adelaide Ramos Rapozo, who is 99 years old. She is the last living sibling of the Joseph Silva Ramos and Filesbertha Vasconcellos clan of 17 children who settled in the Pa'auilo Mauka-Pōhākea area of the Big Island in the early 1900s. In order to assemble this recipe, I had to literally measure each ingredient alongside my mom as she cooked. She cooked by taste. Early in my childhood, whenever Mom cooked this dish, the aroma of garlic and vinegar lingered throughout the house—not to mention out of the house and down the driveway. Even the neighbors knew what we were having for dinner.

Serves 8 to 10

- 5 pounds stew meat
- 3 cloves garlic, minced
- 1 small onion, diced
- 2 tablespoons raw sugar or 1-1/2 packets Splenda
- 1 or 2 small Hawaiian chili peppers
- 1-1/2 cups water
- 1 (6-ounce) can tomato paste
- 3/4 cup white vinegar
- 5 red potatoes, cubed
- 2-1/2 tablespoons rock salt
- 2 carrots, cut into 1-inch chunks

Brown stew meat with garlic and onion in large pot.

Add remaining ingredients. Cook over medium heat for 1-1/2 hours, adding additional water as needed, about 1 to 2 cups.

Sides

What would a turkey dinner be without the stuffing? A barbecue without the potato salad? Side dishes add the finishing touches to a satisfying meal, and here, samplings hail from cuisines around the globe. They include Chinese salty eggs, a vegetarian version of Filipino pancit, a Japanese recipe for shoyu pickled onions, and squid lūʻau to round out a Hawaiian meal.

Grandpa Yun's Famous Stuffing

Submitted by Jody Domingo

Grandpa Yun Young Pang loved his family through his cooking. He not only provided fabulous banquets for hundreds of people, he also made holiday and birthday meals. Even more lovingly, he cooked daily meals after his early shift at the *Honolulu Advertiser* as a pressman. After work, he would grocery shop and then prepare the family's evening meal. As his children grew older (and his family grew larger), sometimes the count for dinner would dwindle due to work and other commitments. This meant that after a full day of work, shopping, and then cooking, Grandpa would phone the various members of his family and invite them to dinner. He always let you know the daily special and let you know that your attendance would be welcomed and appreciated.

Interestingly, out of hundreds of special dishes, Grandpa Yun's stuffing has become a cult favorite among the grandchildren and cousins in the family. This recipe reflects Grandpa's ingenuity in using a Chinese kitchen staple (pork hash) with a special seasoning ingredient that might have come from improvising to avoid another trip to the supermarket.

We prepare and enjoy this stuffing at family gatherings year-round, not just at Thanksgiving and Christmas. I always prepare a batch big enough to feed the entire family, plus enough to freeze. A few family members were initially hesitant to reveal the details of this recipe, but after thinking it over, agreed to share the comfort.

recipe continued on page 116

Serves 8

2 pounds ground pork
1 tablespoon poultry seasoning, or to taste
Pepper, to taste
Garlic salt, to taste
2 medium round onions, diced
6 celery stalks, diced
1 (8-ounce) can sliced mushrooms, drained, or 8 ounces fresh mushrooms, sliced
1 (13-ounce) package cubed Love's stuffing mix with seasoning
3 (3.5-ounce) packages roasted chestnut kernels (available at Palama Market or other Asian markets, in the snack food aisle)
2 (14-ounce) cans chicken broth
1 (10-ounce) bag Lay's original potato chips, crushed in bag
1/2 cup (1 block) butter

In a large pan, brown ground pork with poultry seasoning, salt and pepper until fully cooked. Add diced onions, celery and mushrooms, and sauté till veggies are soft. Slice the block of butter into 1/4- to 1/2-inch pieces and add to pork and vegetables. Stir butter, pork, and vegetables until butter is melted. Add stuffing cubes with seasoning packet and chestnuts. Pour in 2 cans chicken broth and stir well. (For a moister stuffing, add more broth a little at a time.) Add potato chips and stir well.

Stuffing can be eaten at this point, or transfer to baking pan and bake at 350°F for 40 minutes.

Polish Potato Pancakes

Submitted by Helenann Szustek

My recipe for potato pancakes is from my mother-in-law, Rose Szustek. She makes this dish on Easter Sunday, and the whole house smells so wonderful when these pancakes are cooking. This is pure, cozy comfort food at its best. And hey, it is easy to make, too!

Makes 12 (3-inch) pancakes

2 cups baking or all-purpose potatoes
3 large eggs
1-1/2 tablespoons flour
1 tablespoon grated onion
1-1/4 teaspoons salt
4 tablespoons vegetable oil or butter

Grate potatoes in a large bowl. Wrap in a clean towel and wring to squeeze out as much water as possible.

Mix eggs, flour, onion, and salt. Add grated potatoes.

Over medium heat, warm a large skillet with 1/4-inch vegetable oil or melted butter. Place spoonfuls of potato mixture in skillet in batches. Brown until crisp, being careful to reduce heat to prevent burning, 3 to 5 minutes on each side.

Drain briefly on paper towels.

Serve with apple sauce, sour cream, or yogurt.

Salty Eggs

Submitted by Malia Ogoshi

I've always loved salted duck eggs. It's kind of magical that you can transform an egg with salt, water, and thirty days of waiting (no refrigeration needed).

Making this is a scavenger hunt. First you have to find a large, wide-mouth jar. Years ago, you could buy glass gallon mayonnaise jars at Rainbow Drive-In. Now, any Costco jar will work, but you have to decide if you want to eat a gallon of artichoke hearts, pickles, or olives. Next, I go to a local egg producer and buy the largest eggs available. I never did figure out how to find duck eggs so I changed the scavenger hunt requirements.

My mom taught me to add a tablespoon of Chinese tea to the hot water—she says it has antibacterial properties. Later, the tea-stained eggs stand out from the raw ones, which prevents mixing up the two.

When my niece and nephews were little, they called salt eggs "salty eggs"; I use the same term because it reminds me of when they were small fry, happy to eat salt eggs at dinner.

Makes 12 salted eggs

5 cups water
1-1/2 cups Hawaiian salt
1 tablespoon Chinese tea leaves
12 eggs, largest size available

Make a brine: Boil water and stir in salt until dissolved. While still hot, add tea leaves. Set aside and cool.

Wash eggs and place in layers in a wide-mouth glass jar. Cover almost to top of jar with brine. Fill a small sandwich bag with leftover brine and place on top of eggs to keep submerged. Cover jar.

Place jar in a cool place. Check the eggs in 2 weeks. Take one out and boil for 20 minutes. Cool and cut in half (with shell on). Scoop each egg half out of shell with a spoon. Taste test with freshly cooked rice.

If the egg is just right, remove remaining eggs from brine and store in refrigerator for up to one month. If it needs to be saltier, wait another week and test another egg. Leave eggs in brine for up to a month. (If your refrigerated eggs are "expiring," boil them — they will be good for another week or two.)

Serve with jook (congee) or as a side dish.

Squid Lūʻau

Submitted by Jane Kaliko

This recipe was handed down to me by my hānai mother. I have used this recipe for family lūʻau for about 32 years. It's one of those recipes you know by heart and don't measure. I had to really think about how to give measurements for this recipe. In our family, you stand alongside your kupuna and watch how they make their recipe. Doing it so many times, you have the "feel" of the dish. You pass on this knowledge of the recipe in the same way. My kids will ask, "What's the recipe? How much salt? How much sugar?" And my response is, "Stand over here and watch. This much salt, throw a couple of pinches (Hawaiian kind) this much sugar, etc." You know, the "no measure" way of cooking. Mama was real particular about how we cleaned the taro top. She said that the tip of the leaves had the "itchy" so we had to clip it off. (You don't argue with your kupuna!) The stem has to be stripped because it has too much fiber (stringy) and does not cook down. If you use fresh tako, freeze it first to tenderize. Then cook it in some beer, let it cool, then cut up. I have not had a complaint about my lūʻau yet. And yes, people know if I cook the stuff or not.

Serves 8 to 10

- 3 to 4 (supermarket-size) bags fresh taro top
- 1/2 cup Hawaiian salt
- 3 to 4 pounds whole tako (octopus), cooked and chopped
- 2 to 3 cans coconut milk, to taste
- 2 blocks unsalted butter
- 1/2 cup sugar, to taste

Clean taro top. To prevent itching, rub cooking oil on hands before handling the taro. Clip the tips of the leaves. Strip stem like you would celery, and separate leaf and stem.

Bring pot of water to a boil. Add stems to water along with a large pinch of Hawaiian salt. After 5 minutes, start adding leaves by the handful. Add a large pinch of salt after each handful. Press leaves down to fit into pot. They will eventually wilt and melt down. Cook until you can't see the veins of the leaves. Strain leaves in a colander, gently pressing to remove as much liquid as possible. Set aside.

In another large pot, add tako, coconut milk, and unsalted butter. Bring to a slow simmer, then add drained taro tops. Stir well. Add sugar to taste, starting with 1/2 cup.

Simmer lū'au until it starts a slow boil. Stir occasionally from the bottom of the pot to prevent burning.

Serve as a side dish with other lū'au dishes.

Aunty Marine's Meatless Pancit

Submitted by Marine Patao

A few years ago for Thanksgiving, my daughter, a vegetarian, asked me to prepare a meatless dish. I normally used ground pork as the base for my pancit, but I replaced it with dried shiitake mushrooms and it was just as tasty. Since then, I always prepare this dish for family gatherings. A memorable moment was when my niece, Renee, asked me to contribute this pancit for her child's birthday party. I brought 3 pans and zip—everything went.

Serves 4 to 6

- **1 small (1-ounce) package dried shiitake mushrooms, sliced**
- **2 cloves garlic, minced**
- **2 tablespoons cooking oil**
- **2 cans chicken broth**
- **1 bundle long rice**
- **2 packages Canton pancit or wheat noodles (dried)**
- **4 stalks green onion, chopped**
- **1 small carrot, grated**
- **Salt and pepper (optional)**

Soak shiitake mushrooms in water. Drain. Soak long rice in warm water until soft. Drain and cut into 2-inch lengths.

Brown minced garlic in cooking oil. Add shiitake mushrooms and brown for about 2 minutes.

Add 2 cans chicken broth and bring to a boil. Add long rice and stir. Break up dried noodles, then add.

When liquid is absorbed, add green onions and carrot. Add salt and pepper, if using. Toss and serve. If not serving immediately, sprinkle a few tablespoons of chicken broth before serving to keep noodles from sticking.

Auntie Machi's Cucumbers

Submitted by Patricia Ann Tanaka

This recipe came from my oldest sister, Janet Machiko Mau. On Sept. 19, 2006, she passed away. I added ogo, round onion, and a chili pepper to this recipe and entered an ogo (seaweed) contest in 'Ewa Beach. Sam Choy was a judge and said it tasted like an old-style recipe he had as a youngster. I won first place, a $100 prize. But for me, this is a priceless recipe because everyone loves it. Thank you, Machi.

4 to 6 Japanese cucumbers
1 cup shoyu (Aloha is best)
1 cup white vinegar
1 cup sugar
1 tablespoon sesame oil
1 chili pepper, mashed (optional, Hawaiian is best)
1 cup ogo (optional)
1 onion, sliced (optional)

Cut cucumbers in half lengthwise, then into 3/4-inch pieces. (If the cucumber is very thick, cut into fourths.)

Combine shoyu, vinegar, sugar, and sesame oil. Shake and mix well.

Add to cucumbers. Add chili peppers if you like it hot. Add ogo and onion if you like.

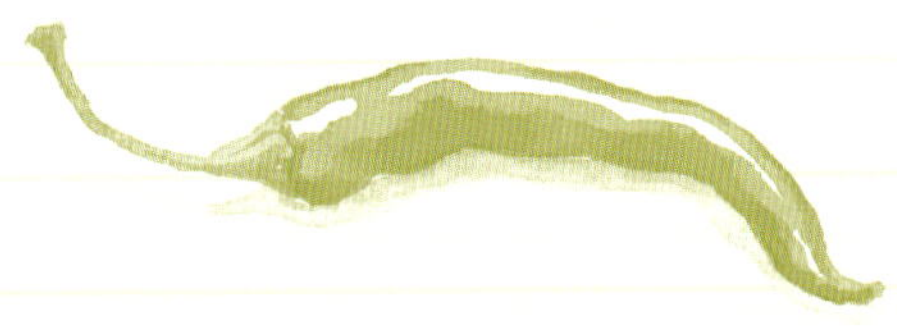

Shoyu Onion

Submitted by Patricia Ann Tanaka

I went to a small restaurant and tasted an onion-type pūpū that was so good. I bought a container and told my family to try it. My family said, "Tūtū, we know you can make this," and the rest is history.

Serves 4

- 2 medium sweet round onions
- 3/4 cup cider vinegar
- 1/2 cup Kikkoman shoyu (very important to use Kikkoman)
- 1/4 cup sugar
- 1/4 cup water
- 1 chili pepper (optional, Hawaiian is best)

Cut onions into medium-size pieces.

Mix the rest of the ingredients, then soak onions in mixture one day and one night. Add chili pepper if you like it hot.

Crozier Potato Salad

Submitted by Karen Crozier

This recipe comes from my wonderful mother-in-law, Mary Kalei Crozier, who learned how to make it from her mother, Anne Wong Leong. The extra eggs in the salad enhance the taste. Mary, now deceased, made this dish on all occasions. When I made it for the first time, my husband grumbled that it didn't taste like his mother's. It became a heated topic between us. He kept saying that his mother used sweet onions, and I disagreed. It was vindication for me when I asked my mother-in-law, who said, "Oh, I just use whatever onion is on sale."

Serves 10 to 15

- 4 to 5 potatoes, boiled or steamed
- 18 large eggs, hardboiled and diced
- 1 large onion, diced
- Salt and pepper, to taste
- 1 to 1-1/2 cups Best Foods mayonnaise

Mix all ingredients in the order listed. Chill overnight and serve the next day.

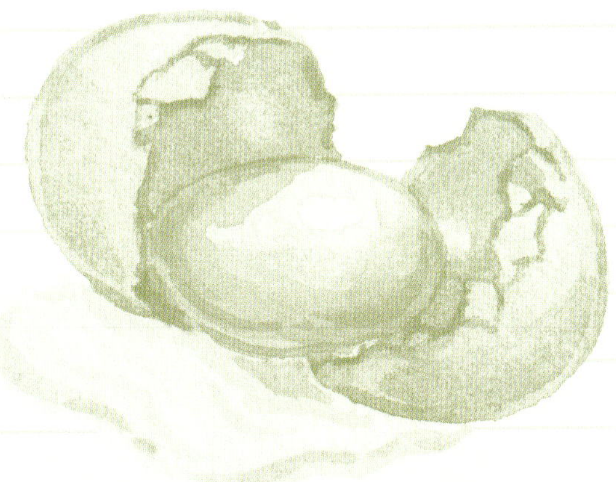

Desserts

There's nothing like finishing off a meal with a sweet treat, and these pages offer something for everyone. Find here recipes for manju, Chinese pretzels, and peanut dumplings as well as mango bars, pineapple pie and chocolate chip cookies. Nostalgic souls can try a spiced orange mold, while coconut lovers won't be able to resist baking up a batch of Samoan coconut rolls. Included are a couple of jelly recipes featuring guava and liliko'i, sweetened not just by fruit and sugar, but by the small-kid memories that accompany them—of picking fruit and working alongside a beloved elder on a labor of love.

Not a Fruitcake

Submitted by Kekoa Yoshida

Most people avoid traditional fruitcake, myself included. That type of fruitcake is made with candied cherries and citrus bits with artificial coloring and preservatives. My dad loved the "local style" fruitcake that was sold at Liberty House during the holiday season. I remember it included, almost exclusively, pineapple and macadamia nuts. It was far better than the traditional fruitcake that we all know so well. My friend introduced a recipe to me that was "as you like it." She said that you can add as much of anything that you desire to this recipe. This gave me the freedom to create a desirable version of this "unpopular holiday brick." My favorite ingredients are pineapple and golden raisins for sweetness, dates and mango for flavor, apricot for tartness, and walnuts for texture. Cranberry is good for tartness too. Papaya and dark raisins also provide sweetness. Macadamia nuts add richness to the loaf. I prefer dried fruits over the processed, candied stuff. The ingredients in this recipe are rounded off. Whatever suits your palate or have on hand will work.

1 cup dates
1/2 cup mangoes
1/2 cup apricots
1/2 cup pineapple
1/2 cup golden raisins
1 cup walnuts
3 cups flour
1/2 pound softened butter (2 blocks)
6 large eggs (room temperature)
2 cups sugar
Pinch salt
1 teaspoon vanilla

Dice dried fruits in a uniform size. Chop walnuts and roast for better flavor. Dust fruits and nuts with 1 tablespoon flour, mix well.

Pre-heat oven to 300°F. Grease and flour pans or use paper liners.

recipe continued on page 130

Cream butter, eggs, sugar, salt, vanilla. Beat flour into wet ingredients until well-combined. Stir in fruits and nuts until well-distributed. Pour into 3 standard loaf pans or 5 mini loaf pans. Cover with foil. Bake for 30 to 35 minutes.

Remove foil. Bake standard loaves for 60 minutes more. Bake mini loaves for an additional 50 minutes. Check with wooden skewer or long toothpick prior to end of baking time. Average total bake time: standard loaf: 95 minutes; mini loaf: 80 minutes. Appearance may be pale to golden brown.

Cool completely before storing or enjoy warm.

Tips: Roast chopped nuts (walnuts or almonds) prior to baking for better flavor and texture. Always add a little salt to enhance sweetness. Dusting fruits and nuts with flour before incorporating into batter prevents them from sinking to the bottom (works for chocolate chips too). Use room temperature eggs, butter, etc. for a better mixture. Try to keep fruits and nuts to no more than 4 cups total. Use disposable pans. They are easier to handle, wrap, and present as gifts. Paper liners work well too. No need to grease paper liners.

EZ Chocolate Chip Cake

Submitted by Kekoa Yoshida

This cake is not too sweet and satisfies the chocoholic. My best friend, Char, loves chocolate to the ends of the earth. Her interpretation of what heaven would look like: a bliss of chocolate everywhere. She proposed an experiment to seek out the perfect chocolate cake: smooth, silky and filled with that decadent substance. So I set out, with lots of tweaking, to create the just-right cake. Not too sweet, not too sharp—and of course quick and easy to make. The result is rich, flavorful, and delightful.

Serves 8

1 cup mini semi-sweet chocolate chips
1 teaspoon flour
3/4 cup vegetable oil
1 cup milk (whole, butter, or skim)
4 large eggs (room temperature)
1 pinch salt
1 box yellow cake mix
1 package instant vanilla pudding mix, unsweetened
4 tablespoons cocoa

Use either three 8x4 loaf pans, five 6x3 mini loaf pans, one tube, or a bundt pan. Preheat oven to 325°F.

Dust chocolate chips with 1 teaspoon flour, set aside.

Grease and flour pans or use paper liners.

Combine wet ingredients. Beat dry ingredients into wet for 3 minutes. Batter will be very thick. Add chocolate chips to batter. Pour evenly into pans.

Bake standard loaves for 45 to 50 minutes. Bake mini loaves for 35 to 40 minutes. Bake tube/bundt for 50 to 60 minutes. Bake times are approximate—ovens vary.

Check loaves with toothpick 5 minutes prior to total baking time. Cool completely before storing.

Pineapple Cream Cheese Pie

Submitted by Janell Europa

Grandma, Juanita Pagan Catania, married young and was a happy homemaker. She smiled all the time. My sister, Ro, and I loved her famous pineapple cream cheese pie. It was the highlight of every special occasion. Once in a while, for no reason at all, she would surprise everyone with this special treat. Eventually my grandparents moved from Hawai'i to California. The tradition continued—whether they came home to visit or we went to them, pineapple cream cheese pie was on the menu.

Now my twin daughters, Sammie and Sydney, help in the kitchen baking chocolate chip cookies, brownies, and of course, Gram's favorite dessert. It's memories in the baking. Now we share this little piece of heaven with you.

Makes 1 (9-inch) pie

Pineapple filling:
1/3 cup sugar
1 can (9 ounces) crushed pineapple (do not drain)
1 tablespoon cornstarch
1 (9-inch) pie shell, unbaked

Cream cheese mixture:
8 ounces cream cheese, softened
1/2 cup sugar
1/2 teaspoon salt
4 eggs
1/2 cup milk
1/2 teaspoon vanilla

Preheat oven to 400°F. For the pineapple filling, combine all the ingredients and cook on low heat, stirring constantly until thick and clear. Let cool completely then evenly spread into pie shell.

To make the cream cheese mixture, blend cream cheese with sugar and salt. Add in eggs. Add milk and vanilla and mix thoroughly.

Pour over pineapple layer. Bake for 10 minutes then lower temperature to 325°F and bake for another 45 minutes.

Pineapple Cream Pie

Submitted by Elissa Dulce

My husband is from Tonga and LOVES pineapple served in any shape or form. Twenty-five years ago, I found this recipe and, according to him, I had discovered gold. He would ask me to make it all the time, but we usually ate the pie at our family Christmas gathering or on other special occasions. Although it's not a quick dessert, the time put into it is well worth the wait.

Serves 8

Pineapple filling:
1/3 cup firmly packed cornstarch
4 egg yolks
1 tablespoon water
1 (20-ounce) can crushed pineapple
1 cup sugar
1/4 teaspoon salt
2 cups whole milk
2 tablespoons butter
1 teaspoon vanilla

Crust:
3/4 cup butter
1/2 cup chopped nuts
1-1/2 cups flour

Cream cheese filling:
1 (8-ounce) package cream cheese, softened
1/2 cup confectioner's sugar, sifted
1/2 teaspoon vanilla
1/3 cup chopped walnuts
1/3 cup reserved pineapple, drained

Topping:
1 cup whipped cream
1/4 cup confectioner's sugar, sifted

Preheat oven to 375°F.

To make filling, combine corn starch, egg yolks, and water in a small bowl. Set aside.

Measure 1 cup pineapple and juice. Drain juice. Reserve remaining pineapple.

Combine sugar, salt, milk, and drained pineapple in saucepan. Cook on medium heat and stir until mixture almost comes to a boil, then reduce heat to low. Add egg yolk mixture slowly, stirring constantly, until thickened.

Add butter and vanilla. Remove from heat. Cover with waxed paper. Refrigerate 30 minutes, stirring once or twice.

For crust, mix ingredients and press evenly into 9x13-inch pan. Bake for 15 minutes until golden brown. Cool completely.

To make cream cheese filling, combine cream cheese and confectioner's sugar. Beat with fork until blended and smooth. Add vanilla, walnuts, and pineapple. Mix well.

Spread over bottom of cooled, baked shell. Cover with pineapple filling.

For topping, spread whipped cream sweetened with confectioner's sugar. Garnish with remaining drained, crushed pineapple and more nuts. Refrigerate until ready to serve.

Mango Bars

Submitted by Lillian Kashiwabara

This recipe started out as an apple bar recipe, but my love for our local produce—especially Island mangoes—gave me the idea to replace the apples with mangoes. You can substitute the mangoes with other fruits as well, including peaches, prunes, apricots, etc. This recipe is special to our family because it's a delicious and somewhat healthier snack than store-bought fruit or cereal bars.

Makes 4 dozen bars

Crust:
2 cups flour
1/2 cup sugar
1 cup butter

Filling:
4 cups chopped mango
3/4 cup sugar
1/3 cup water
1 teaspoon lemon juice
3 tablespoons cornstarch, dissolved in 3 tablespoons water

Topping:
2 cups quick oats
1/4 cup flour
1/2 cup sugar
2/3 cup butter

Preheat oven to 350°F. To make crust, combine flour and sugar in a bowl. Cut in butter. Press into 9x13-inch pan. Bake 7 to 10 minutes, until lightly browned.

For filling, combine mangoes, sugar, water, and lemon juice in a pan. Cook about 10 minutes, until mangoes are tender. Stir in cornstarch slurry and cook until thickened. Cool slightly. Pour over prepared crust.

To make topping, combine oats, flour, and sugar. Cut in butter. Sprinkle over mango mixture. Bake 50 minutes. Cool and cut into bars.

Chocolate Chip Squares

Submitted by Leslie Ann Hayashi

In college, one of my friends introduced me to the chocolate chip squares her mother sent in care packages. They quickly became my favorite treat.

When I had my own children, I made this chocolate lover's recipe and it quickly became a favorite at soccer potlucks, bake sales and various get-togethers.

When my sons wanted to buy something special, they would bake and sell the squares. Justin, my older son, baked the squares while Taylor stood outside, selling them for 50 cents. One day, Taylor came rushing into house, excited that he had sold all the squares to a nice woman in a Mercedes. He held up a $100 bill! Aghast, I ran outside to find the woman and return the money, but she was gone.

Although my sons are now in law school and college, both are fondly remembered for this recipe. Teachers have even asked for it. So here's the recipe from our house to yours—enjoy!

Serves 8 to 10

1-1/3 cup butter
1 cup white sugar
1 cup brown sugar
2 eggs
2 teaspoons vanilla
3 cups flour
1 teaspoon baking soda
1 teaspoon salt
32 ounces (or more) chocolate chips (the more you add, the more decadent it is!)

Preheat oven to 375°F.

Beat butter, sugars, eggs, and vanilla thoroughly.

In a separate bowl, combine flour, baking soda, and salt. Blend both mixtures. Add chocolate chips. Spread dough in an ungreased 13x9-inch pan. Bake 40 to 45 minutes. The center may take a little longer to cook, so test by inserting a toothpick; it should come out clean.

Cool and cut into squares.

Note: A half-recipe may be baked in a 9-inch square pan for 20 to 25 minutes.

Walnut Cupcakes

Submitted by Fern Yamane

In the '70s I was living in 'O'ōkala on the Big Island with my mom, Granny, my husband, Glenn, and our children, Jan and Lee. Granny was always into buying gadgets. One day out pops this brand new Vitamix mixer with a shiny stainless steel bowl. It was a craze in the '70s. Well, I tested it with this bundt cake recipe that I got from a friend at school. I began to measure each ingredient from the top of the page, working my way down. At the end of the ingredient list I read the instructions, and yikes, the walnuts, cinnamon, and sugar were for the topping! I had mixed them all up! All I could do was push the start button on the mixer. I baked it and my "mistake" walnut cake was a big hit with my family. I usually use a 7x11 cake pan to get the cake taller. Now, my youngest daughter, Ai, is our baker in the family. She is always dreaming up new ideas for her keiki at Noelani Elementary School.

Makes 24 cupcakes

- 3/4 cup water
- 3/4 cup popcorn oil
- 1 teaspoon vanilla
- 4 extra large eggs
- 1 box (18.25 ounces) Duncan Hines butter cake mix
- 1 (5.1-ounce) box JELL-O vanilla instant pudding
- 1 teaspoon cinnamon
- 1 cup chopped walnuts
- 1 (13.5 ounce) Easy Frost Cream Cheese Frosting, for decorating

Preheat oven to 350°F.

Mix water, oil, vanilla, and eggs. Add remaining ingredients. Mix on medium speed 2 minutes. Pour batter into 24 cupcake liners in muffin pan. Bake for 20 minutes. Insert a toothpick in the middle of one of the cupcakes. If it comes out clean, the cupcakes are done.

Note: If you would like to make a cake instead of cupcakes, a 7x11-inch cake pan can be used. Bake for 45 to 50 minutes.

Grandma Alice's World-Famous Bran Muffins

Submitted by Dot Mason

My mom, "Grandma Alice," had 26 grandchildren and 34 great-grandchildren by the time she passed away at age 94. She loved to have lots of them around and loved to cook in big batches. Also, she felt this was good, healthy stuff. Her granddaughters have kept this recipe moving through the family and friends.

This is a good one for busy Hawai'i families because you can make up a big batch and keep it in the refrigerator up to two weeks. You can add nuts or raisins for variety.

Makes 3 to 4 dozen

2 cups Nabisco or Miller's bran
2 cups boiling water
1/2 cup shortening
2-1/4 cups sugar
4 eggs
5 cups flour
2 teaspoons salt
1 quart buttermilk
5 teaspoons baking soda
4 cups Kellog's All-Bran

Put 2 cups Nabisco bran in a bowl—pour 2 cups boiling water over and set aside.

Cream shortening, sugar, and eggs. Add other ingredients, including Nabisco bran, and add All-Bran last. Mix well. Refrigerate overnight.

To bake muffins: Preheat oven to 400°F. Line muffin tin with paper cups and fill each cup 3/4 full of batter. Bake 12 to 15 minutes.

Notes: Return extra batter to refrigerator to use as needed. A commercial-size mayonnaise jar is a perfect container. Nuts, dates, and/or raisins may be mixed into the batter.

THE Crispiest Chocolate Chip Cookie

Submitted by Lynette Yuen

Finding THE crispiest cookie recipe is very difficult. Most recipes are crispy on the outside but chewy on the inside. Nani Carroll at Mah Jong suggested using unsalted butter when I made these cookies. I also substituted some brown sugar and refrigerated the dough for several days. Voilà—THE crispiest cookie recipe was born. It's a contest winner, and all who have tried them loved them.

Makes about 3 dozen

- 2 cups flour
- 1 teaspoon baking soda
- 1 teaspoon salt
- 1 cup unsalted butter
- 1 cup white sugar
- 1/2 cup light brown sugar
- 1 egg
- 1 teaspoon vanilla
- 1 package semi-sweet chocolate chips
- 1 cup nuts

In a bowl, mix flour, baking soda, and salt.

In another large bowl, cream the butter and sugars, then add egg and vanilla. Stir flour mixture into butter mixture and add chocolate chips and nuts.

Refrigerate for several days until the dough is stiff.

When ready to bake, preheat oven to 350°F. Drop dough by the teaspoonful on greased or foil-lined cookie sheets. Bake for 25 minutes.

Char's Chocolate Crinkles

Submitted by Kristy Kimura

As long as I can remember, it was my mom's chocolate crinkles for Christmas gift giving. The "chosen few" family and friends wait patiently each holiday for their prize of chocolate. These are treasures, labors of love, as making them consumes an entire weekend. But the heartwarming compliments make it worth every minute.

Our mom usually chooses the weekend after Thanksgiving to collect the ingredients and start the process. On Thursday evening we measure, mix and store the batter—at least ten batches to be refrigerated till Saturday! The chocolate dough must be very firm, otherwise we'd have a melted mess.

On baking day the fun starts. Daddy scoops out the dough, my sister Kelli rolls the batter into 1-inch balls, Kari rolls the balls in a bowl of powdered sugar and places them on the baking sheets. Mom monitors the oven. My job is to remove the cookies from the cookie sheets to cool. Charlie, our dog, licks the floor to make sure no powdered sugar goes to waste.

My sisters and I run to the neighbors to share our holiday treats while they are fresh out of the oven. After dinner, Mom stays up past midnight to pack all the cookies for gift giving. On Sunday we are out of the house first thing in the morning to deliver our holiday crinkles. We return just in time for dinner. Until next year, we have 12 months of rest!

recipe continued on page 144

Makes 72 cookies

- 2 cups sugar
- 1/2 cup oil
- 4 squares unsweetened chocolate, melted
- 4 eggs
- 2 cups flour
- 2 teaspoons baking powder
- 1/2 teaspoon salt
- 2 teaspoons vanilla
- Powdered sugar, for coating cookies

In a large mixing bowl, combine all ingredients. Cover and refrigerate 2 days, until very firm. Or for quicker cooking, freeze.

Preheat oven to 350°F. Shape dough into 1-inch balls and roll each ball in powdered sugar to coat. Place on baking sheets about 1 inch apart. Bake 8 to 10 minutes.

Crunchy Jumble Cookies

Submitted by Lolly Saari

A soccer mom brought these to a game when my daughter played. It is a family favorite. Because it calls for so many ingredients, I make these only once or twice a year. It is a well-appreciated gift.

Makes 4 dozen

- 5 cups flour (3 cups white/regular + 2 cups whole wheat)
- 2 teaspoons baking soda
- 1/4 teaspoon salt
- 2-1/2 cups Quaker Oats (1-minute type OK)
- 3 cups semi-sweet chocolate chips
- 1 cup chopped walnuts
- 1 cup chopped pecans
- 1 cup shredded coconut
- 1/2 cup raw sunflower seeds
- 1/2 cup raw pumpkin seeds
- 1 cup dried cranberries
- 1 cup dried li hing mui mango, chopped
- 1/2 cup wheat germ (Honey crunch)-optional
- 2 cups butter, softened
- 2 cups white sugar
- 1 cup brown sugar
- 2 eggs
- 2 teaspoons vanilla

Preheat oven 275°F. Combine flour, baking soda, and salt. Set aside.

Combine oats, chocolate chips, walnuts, pecans, coconut, sunflower seeds, pumpkin seeds, cranberries, li hing mango, and wheat germ. Set aside.

Beat together butter and sugars until fluffy. Add eggs and vanilla to butter/sugar mixture and beat. Add flour mixture and beat. Add oat mixture. (Dough will be stiff.)

Shape rounded tablespoonfuls into balls and place on ungreased cookie sheets (about 20 to 22 cookies per sheet). Gently flatten. Bake for 50 minutes or until light golden brown. Flip cookies to cool. Keep in airtight container.

Grandma's Homemade Apple Rolls

Submitted by Gwen Nakamura

As the assistant University of Hawai'i band director at all of the UH athletic games and functions, Prep Bowls, marching band and concerts, I am busy as anyone. But I find solace in planning Sunday dinner for my family, which includes my mom, my brother Neal and his family, my sister JoAnn, my niece Drew, and her friends. And doggies are allowed to attend the party with my Yuki, a purebred Spitz. Oh Happy Days! Besides cooking for Yuki and walking her daily, I love cooking, as is reflected by the number of cookbooks I collect, read, and re-read. My pride and joy, besides Yuki, is my special room with shelves of cookbooks. My mom is amazed.

This recipe came from my Grandmother Nakamura who has now passed. She was from Hilo, and every summer as a child, I would stay with her and my grandfather for a few weeks. It was an older home with a furo in the basement. What a wonderful time we had keeping each other company.

I would help them and learn all about baking, crocheting, knitting, and caring for their orchids and anthuriums. Every morning my grandmother would make breakfast for my grandfather, who would eat the same thing: toast and one soft-boiled egg. My grandmother would make the apple rolls on the weekends as a special treat. I could smell them from my room on Saturdays. It became a family favorite, and I would eat them every Saturday with my grandfather. When it was time for me to return home to O'ahu, my grandmother would send back a few dozen apple rolls with me. Now I make them and will carry on the tradition.

recipe continued on page 148

Serves 6

2 cups flour
2 tablespoons sugar
4 teaspoons baking powder
1/2 teaspoon salt
6 tablespoons shortening
2/3 cup milk
1 egg
4 tablespoons sugar
1/2 teaspoon cinnamon
2 apples, peeled, cored and thinly sliced (Fuji and Golden Delicious; or Granny Smith for a tart flavor)

Glaze:
1 cup powdered sugar
Lemon, few drops (either fresh lemon or from concentrate)
Hot water

Preheat oven to 425°F. Sift together the flour, sugar, baking powder, and salt. Cut in shortening. Add milk and egg. The batter will be somewhat sticky and doughy.

Divide dough into 12 portions. Roll each portion out or flatten.

Combine the sugar and cinnamon. Toss apple slices into the sugar/cinnamon mix. Place a few apple slices on the dough and roll up. Put into lined muffin pans.

Bake for 20 minutes. While baking, make the glaze. Combine powdered sugar, lemon, and a little hot water to achieve the consistency of glaze.

Once the rolls are baked, drizzle the glaze on top. Eat while still warm.

Panipopo
(Samoan Coconut Rolls)

Submitted by Jenni and Eddie Maiava

Panipopos are a sweet treat. Whenever my husband, Eddie, is homesick for Samoa, he asks me to make these coconut rolls. They are a favorite dessert of our kids, nieces, and nephews. Whenever our relatives are in town or over for dinner, they request panipopos for dessert.

Serves 8 to 10

1 cup evaporated milk, very warm
1 tablespoon yeast
1 tablespoon sugar
1/4 cup sugar
3 eggs
1 teaspoon salt
3-1/2 cups flour, plus 1 more cup as needed
1/2 cup melted butter

Coconut Sauce:
2 cans coconut milk
3/4 to 1 cup sugar
3 tablespoons cornstarch dissolved in 1/4 cup water

Combine milk with yeast and 1 tablespoon sugar. Let sit until foamy.

Mix together: 1/4 cup sugar, eggs, salt, flour, and butter. Add yeast mixture; knead until smooth. Add up to 1 cup more flour as needed, just enough to make dough smooth and elastic. Let rise one hour; punch down. Let rise another 30 minutes. Shape into rolls and place in large pan. Let rise while you make the coconut sauce.

To make sauce: Combine coconut milk and sugar in saucepan and heat, stirring to dissolve sugar. Add cornstarch mixture, stirring constantly, until it begins to thicken. Pour over rolls. Let sit 15 minutes.

Preheat oven to 375°F. Bake rolls 20 to 25 minutes, until golden brown.

Quick Cinnamon Rolls

Submitted by Brenda Dickinson

Just thinking about my dad's homemade cinnamon rolls brings back memories of my childhood, waking up to a delicious smell drifting through the house and the anticipation of enjoying the sweet rolls for breakfast. This recipe originated from the cookbook *All About Home Baking*, published in 1933 by General Foods Corp. The cookbook was given to my mother by her landlady in 1961, while my mom was attending college in Nebraska.

When my mother returned to Hawai'i the cookbook become one of her treasures, along with this recipe, which had became my dad's specialty.

Makes 12 rolls

2-1/2 cups sifted cake flour
2-1/2 teaspoons baking powder
1/2 teaspoon salt
3 tablespoons butter or shortening
3/4 cup milk

Filling:
2 tablespoons butter
1/3 cup brown sugar, firmly packed
1/2 teaspoon cinnamon
1/2 cup currants or raisins

Topping:
1/4 cup butter
1/4 cup brown sugar

recipe continued on page 152

Preheat oven to 450°F.

Sift flour once, measure, add baking powder and salt, and sift again. Cut in shortening. Add milk all at once and stir carefully until all flour is dampened. Then stir vigorously until mixture forms a cohesive dough and follows spoon around bowl.

Turn out immediately on slightly floured board and knead 30 seconds. Roll 1/4-inch thick.

To make filling: Cream together butter, sugar, and cinnamon; spread over dough and sprinkle with currants. Roll up as you would a jelly roll. Cut in 1-1/4-inch slices.

To make topping: Melt butter in 8x8 inch pan. Add brown sugar and mix well. Place rolls in pan, cut-side down. Bake 15 minutes; reduce heat to 350°F and bake 15 to 20 minutes longer. Remove rolls from pan and turn over to serve.

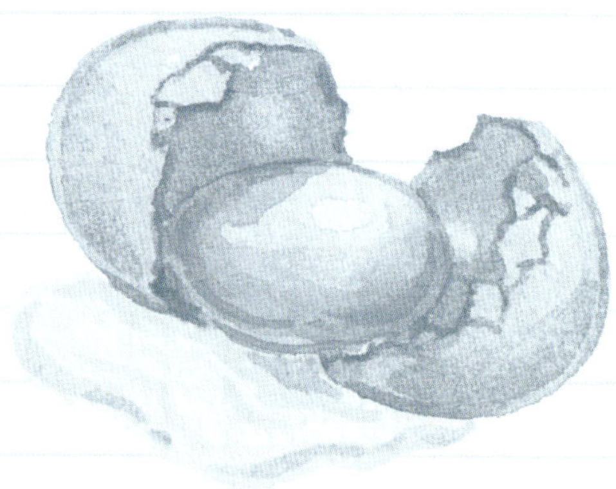

Karamachiya
(Okinawan Chocolate Crêpes)

Submitted by Charlotte M. Arakaki

My maternal grandmother created this snack after coming to Hawai'i from Okinawa. Like many local dishes, it melded an ingredient known from her homeland (mochiko) with a new one (cocoa powder) that she became familiar with here. Instead of using standardized measuring cups or spoons she used her sight, touch, and taste to prepare this batter, which was consistently delicious. Eventually, we measured the ingredients because we lacked Grandma's skills.

This snack has been enjoyed by four generations—that of my grandmother, mother, my own, and now my son.

Serves 10

3/4 cup flour
3/4 cup mochiko
3/4 cup sugar
3/4 cup sweetened cocoa powder (such as Nesquik)
2 cups milk
2 eggs
2 teaspoons vanilla
Butter to grease skillet

Mix flour, mochiko, sugar, and cocoa powder. Add milk, eggs, and vanilla. Mix until smooth.

Heat a skillet on medium-low and grease generously with butter. Pour 1/2 cup onto skillet. When bubbles appear, flip over. Cook until done. Roll up like a crepe.

Okinawan Sweet Potato Ohagi

Submitted by Grant Sato

My grandma is a lover of anything purple, so when it comes to home gardening, Okinawan sweet potato is a must. The only problem is that harvest is once a year, so you must come up with creative ways to extend its shelf life. Grandma knew that ohagi was a favorite of mine, so she decided to add mashed sweet potato to the an (bean) filling. This became a hit and a family standard for holiday get-togethers.

If anyone asks her the story to her ohagi, she will insist she created it out of necessity. The mashed sweet potato stretches the expensive an, and without it, her "mochi crazy" grandson would bankrupt her over the cost of an. Grandma continues to remind me of a family trip to Kaua'i when, as a three-year-old, I supposedly stole everyone's mochi and devoured the morsels. I'll always have room for ohagi made with love.

Makes 12 pieces

2 cups mochi rice
1/2 cup calrose rice
3 cups water
2 medium Okinawan sweet potatoes
1 can tsubushi an
Granulated sugar, to taste

Combine the mochi and calrose rice in a bowl and wash thoroughly, making sure to drain all the water out. Drain the rice for 3 hours.

Place rice and 3 cups of water in a rice cooker and cook.

Place the sweet potato in a steamer and steam for 40 minutes. (You could also steam the rice, but be sure to stack the rice above the potato to ensure it won't be discolored by falling purple liquid.)

Form cooked rice into 12 egg-shaped bullets.

Mash the sweet potato and mix in the tsubushi an. Add sugar to taste.

recipe continued on page 156

Place a 12-inch square piece of plastic wrap on a plate and place 1/2 cup of the potato-an mixture in the center. Spread into an oval about 1/4-inch thick and place the rice bullet in the center. Carefully lift up the edges of the wrap and evenly mold the sweet potato mixture around the rice to form the ohagi. Serve at room temperature.

Umushi Manju

Submitted by Tokie Ching

Whenever my late brother, Taka, came home after his baseball game, Mom would make his favorite dessert—extra big, purple potato manju. Taka's face would light up and he smiled his biggest smile even when he smelled the manju in the steamer. He enjoyed every bite and looked so content after devouring his favorite dessert.

Makes about 3 dozen

2-1/2 cups flour
1 cup Bisquick
Pinch salt
2-1/2 teaspoons baking powder
3 egg whites
3/4 cup milk
1 cup sugar
1/4 cup salad oil

Potato mixture:
4 to 5 medium Okinawan sweet potatoes
1/4 cup condensed milk
Dash of salt

In a large bowl, sift the flour, Bisquick, salt and baking powder. In a separate bowl, mix the egg whites with milk. Add sugar and salad oil. Mix well.

Add wet ingredients to dry ingredients. Mix well. Let stand for 10 to 15 minutes.

To prepare the potato filling, boil the potatoes in a pot of water with enough water to cover. Cook for about 30 minutes, or until you can poke a chopstick into a potato easily.

When cooled, peel and mash. Add condensed milk and salt and mix until creamy. Shape a tablespoon of filling into a round ball. Repeat using all the filling.

With floured hands, break off a piece of dough the size of a ping pong ball. Round the dough in the palm of your hands and flatten it to a 2-1/2-inch diameter.

Place a ball of filling into the center of the dough.

Fold the edges of the dough over the potato and twist it to seal. Steam in a steamer for 15 minutes.

Yakimanju
(Baked Manju with Mashed Lima Bean Filling)

Submitted by Harry H. Matsuno

This recipe was from my grandmother who was from Japan. The recipe was handed down to my mother, and I learned it from her. It is a time-consuming two-day process and my wife has no interest in the process. Since my parents were devout Buddhists I maintain their butsudan at my home even though I am not a member of the Buddhist church. I bake the manju on New Year's and on the dates of their deaths in September and October of each year. I also share the 120 to 130 manju that I bake with family and friends. The first time they ate the manju they were surprised to see a lima bean filling rather than the azuki bean.

Makes 120 to 130 silver dollar-size pieces

Filling:
2 (16-ounce) packages boiled, mashed lima beans
6 cups water (to boil beans)
3 cups sugar

recipe continued on page 160

Wrapper:

1-1/2 cups butter-flavored Crisco

1-1/2 cups sugar

5 eggs, well-beaten (reserve 1 tablespoon to moisten and seal manju)

1 teaspoon vanilla

4 cups flour

1-1/2 teaspoons baking powder

1-1/2 teaspoons baking soda

1-1/2 teaspoons table salt

1 package sesame seeds

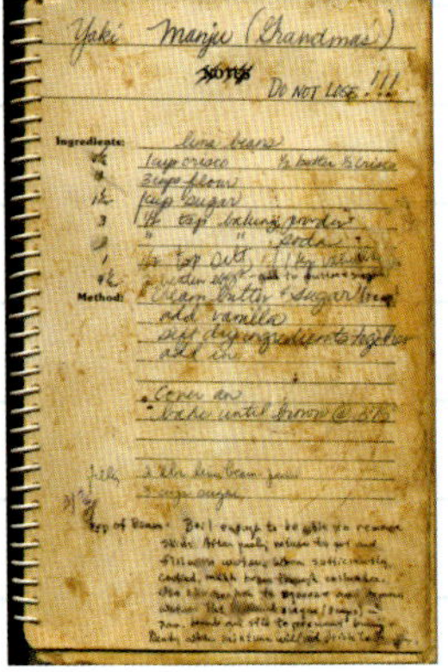

Prepare filling: Mom would boil the lima beans and remove the skins while still hot. I found that the easiest way is to place the lima beans in a pot of hot water and let stand for three or four hours. By then the water has cooled and the skin can be removed from the beans.

Boil the beans until they start to fall apart. Place a sieve on a cheesecloth. Place a couple of cups of lima beans into strainer and using the back of a ladle, press the beans through the sieve. Wring the cheesecloth so the water is removed. Repeat the process until finished.

Place pot on stove with half of the lima beans and 3 cups of sugar. When mixture thickens, add the rest of the lima beans and stir to keep from scorching. If the mixture does not stick to your finger, it is ready. Let stand for a couple of hours until it cools and can be made into balls. Place in refrigerator overnight. This helps to dry out the lima bean filling.

Prepare wrapper: Cream Crisco and sugar. Add beaten eggs, then vanilla. Sift all dry ingredients, then add to wet ingredients. Mix all ingredients and place on cutting board with plenty of flour on the surface.

Preparation: Pinch off a piece of dough, flatten out, and place a ball in the middle. Work with the dough until the ball is evenly covered, and place on cookie sheet about 1/2 inch apart. When sheet is filled, dab the manju with beaten egg. Sprinkle with sesame seed and bake at 350°F for 15 minutes.

Steamed An Mochi

Submitted by Patsy Iha

I got this recipe from my mother-in-law—mochi with an, wrapped in a ti leaf and steamed. It was a recipe that she and her mother used. I made some adjustments to Grandma's recipe: I added sugar to the mochi and used banana leaves instead of ti leaves. It became a family favorite because it's not too sweet and has real mochi texture. At first, I made it only for New Year's but now I make it often.

Makes 20 to 24 pieces

Banana leaves, washed and cut in 2-inch x 5-1/2-inch pieces
Cooking spray or oil, to grease leaves
1 cup tsubu an (coarse sweetened red bean paste)
2 cups mochiko (sweet rice flour)
1/3 cup flour
3 tablespoons vegetable oil
3 tablespoons sugar
1 cup water

Spray or oil one side of each piece of banana leaf.

Roll teaspoons of an into balls. Set aside.

Combine mochiko, flour, oil, and sugar in a bowl. Add water and mix until smooth. Form dough into balls, flatten, and place a ball of an in the center.

Wrap mochi around the an and pinch edges together to seal. (Keep hands damp with cold water to keep mochi from sticking.) Wrap each mochi in a piece of oiled banana leaf (mochi will not be completely covered). Arrange bundles in a single layer in the top basket of a steamer. Do not stack them. The leaf part of the bundles can touch, but don't let the exposed mochi touch. It will expand. Steam over simmering water for 18 minutes.

Note: Ti leaves can be used instead of banana leaves. For softer mochi, add 1 to 2 tablespoons water to the batter. This batter will be a little more difficult to handle (if batter becomes too soft, add a little more mochiko).

Popo's Sweet Peanut Dumplings

(Dow Low)

Submitted by Jamie Cheng

In our family, Popo is the matriarch that brings everyone together, and her sticky, sweet dow low accomplishes just that. This dish is not reserved for special occasions. It can be whipped up in minutes using just a few ingredients from the pantry. Dow low is still one of our most treasured family recipes because everyone can take part in its preparation. Sometimes after dinner, Popo will announce that she's making dow low. Ears perk up, the television turns off, and everyone gathers in the kitchen. A combination of tiny hands and wrinkled hands all work together to form the sticky dough into dumplings. And after the last ball is rolled, everyone gathers around the table as Popo serves the beloved peanut dumplings.

Makes 60 to 80 bite-size dumplings

Dough:

2 cups water
1 pound mochiko (glutinous rice flour)

Peanut mix:

1-1/2 cups dry roasted unsalted peanuts
1/2 cup sugar
1/2 cup kinako

To make the dough, add water to the mochiko and combine until a sticky dough forms. The dough should be moist enough to bind together but dry enough to hold its shape, like play dough. Adjust by adding water or mochiko.

Roll into bite-size balls about the size of a teaspoon. Place on waxed paper.

For the peanut mix, put all the ingredients in a food processor and pulse until all the peanuts are crushed. Transfer the mixture to a shallow bowl.

Bring a small pot of water to a boil. Boil the dumplings in small batches of about 12. The dumplings are cooked when they start to float.

Remove with a strainer and immediately roll them in the peanut mixture. Remove to a plate and serve while warm.

Buko Salad
(Filipino Ambrosia Fruit Salad)

Submitted by Susan M. Segawa

It's been about 25 years since I first stumbled upon this recipe for ambrosia salad with a twist. When I started taking it to gatherings, it was a hit and continues to be a favorite. This dessert is addicting, and it seems everyone just can't get enough of it so I make a lot. "Buko" means coconut in Filipino.

Serves 6 to 8

- **1 large can fruit cocktail or tropical salad chunks (available at Sam's Club)**
- **1 bottle kaong (palm nut in heavy syrup)**
- **1 bottle coconut or pineapple gel (in syrup)**
- **1 bottle macapuno strings (coconut strings in heavy syrup)**
- **2 pints whipping cream**

Drain fruit well. Rinse and drain kaong, coconut or pineapple gel, and coconut strings (separate strings).

Mix all ingredients in a large container. Chill well and serve.

Grandma's Backyard Guava Jelly

Submitted by Grant Sato

I can remember picking guavas and making jelly with Grandma from "small kid days." Grandma was the tall one back then, and my job was to pick the ripe guavas from the lower branches and quickly retrieve the ones that grandma dropped as she reached up to pick the fruit from the top of the tree. Fruit picking in the backyard was always the most exciting task for me. Only now do I realize that my playtime with Grandma doubled as cooking lessons. Thirty-five years later, Grandma and I continue to pick guava and make jelly together, although our roles have changed—now I pick the guavas from the top of the tree, and she just picks what she can reach while waving "hi" to the neighbors.

Makes 4 (1-cup) jars

10 cups ripe strawberry guava, washed with stems removed
3-1/2 cups granulated sugar
1/2 pound paraffin wax

Crush guavas by hand or use a potato masher.

Place in a medium-size pot and simmer for 20 minutes, then turn heat up high and boil for another 10 minutes, stirring constantly to prevent burning.

Line a colander with cheesecloth and place it inside a large bowl. Pour cooked guava into the cheesecloth and allow it to strain for 1 hour. Do not force guava through the cheesecloth; this will create a cloudy jelly. This will yield about 2-1/2 cups of guava juice.

Place juice in a medium saucepan and add sugar. Bring to a quick boil, then skim the "scum" from the surface.

When bubbles become large, test the mixture by dipping a clean spoon into the center of the pot. If the mixture quickly sheets off the spoon, continue to cook. When it falls off in drops that run together, the jelly is ready.

recipe continued on page 168

Place jelly into sterilized jars and top with paraffin. The hot jelly will melt the wax and allow it to cover the jelly completely.

When the jelly cools and the wax hardens, cover with lids and store at room temperature. Once the jar is opened and wax is removed, it must be refrigerated.

Mom's Homemade Liliko'i Jelly

Submitted by Yvonne Chun Izumi

My mom, Mildred Tam Chun, is remembered for her original treats and liliko'i jelly. From her own liliko'i vine, Mom harvested more than 100 fruit to prepare yummy treats. I remember picking liliko'i as a child in our Mānoa yard. Scooping the fresh pulp and straining the juice was a time for bonding with mom. Sweet liliko'i fragrance was everywhere, and we made liliko'i jelly, candies, pies, cakes, frostings, and more. Everyone loved receiving jelly at Christmas because it was home grown, straight from the vine and made with lots of love.

Makes 12 (4- to-6-ounce) jars

- 6-1/2 cups sugar
- 1-1/2 cups water
- 1 (6-ounce) bottle Certo pectin
- 1-1/2 cups fresh liliko'i concentrate
- 1 (8-ounce) block paraffin wax

Place sugar and water in a large saucepan and mix well. On high heat, bring to a rolling boil and cook for 1 minute, stirring constantly.

Remove from heat and immediately stir in Certo. Add liliko'i juice and mix well. Pour quickly into sterilized jars. Cover at once with 1/8-inch hot paraffin.

Refrigerate jelly.

Spiced Orange Mold

Submitted by Sammye Love

As my family had always served JELL-O salads for holidays, I decided to look for an easy and different salad the first year I was married. I settled on this one because I loved the taste and how it went with turkey or ham. After 44 years, I still love the ease of it and have improved upon it, too. The original recipe called for a 3-ounce can of oranges—I use a 15-ounce can. I also use sugar-free JELL-O and place my whole cloves in a tea ball so I don't have to strain them out. Also, instead of using a mold, I make it in a Corning Ware dish and serve it in the same dish.

Serves 6 to 8

1 (15-ounce) can mandarin oranges
1/4 teaspoon salt
6-inch cinnamon stick
1/2 teaspoon whole cloves
1 (6-ounce) package sugar-free orange JELL-O
1-3/4 cups of water and 2 cups of cold water (separated)
3 tablespoons lemon juice
1/2 cup broken pecans

Drain oranges, reserving syrup in measuring cup. Add water to syrup to make 1-3/4 cups of liquid. Combine syrup with salt, cinnamon, and cloves in saucepan. Cover, bring to boil, then reduce heat and simmer 10 minutes. Remove from heat, let stand, covered, for 10 minutes. Strain. (Cloves may be placed in a tea ball to make them easier to remove.)

Dissolve gelatin in hot strained liquid. Add 2 cups cold water and lemon juice. Chill until partially set.

Stir in oranges and nuts. (If desired pour into a mold.) Chill until firm.

Remembering

So much of Hawai'i's culinary tradition comes from 'ohana founded and operated restaurants, where all family members participated—from children just old enough to work, to grandmas watching the cash register. In environments ranging from hole-in-the-walls to mid-size and large restaurants, family recipes handed down over the generations are the centerpiece of the larger menu to be enjoyed by everyone.

Here are our favorite family restaurant recipes—a befitting dessert ending for this culinary adventure through our 'ohana.

The Willows Curry

Submitted by Ray Orozco who worked at The (Original) Willows

In the 1940s, Emma Hausten and her family dreamed of offering the finest in gracious hospitality that would mimic the relaxing atmosphere of home ... the kind of place reserved for friends and family to gather and share the important moments of the day. On July 4, 1944, the Hausten ‘ohana realized their dream by opening The Willows, a restaurant where everyone was welcomed with aloha.

Today, a visit to The Willows is a step back to a time when guests were greeted by the melodious sound of Hawaiian music, the fragrance of plumeria, and a sweet komomai—welcome. Here is where curry, mango chutney, and coconut sky high pie became famous.

Curry Sauce:

3 garlic cloves, minced
1/4 cup fresh chopped ginger
2 cups finely chopped onions
6 tablespoons clarified butter
3 teaspoons salt
3 teaspoons sugar
3 tablespoons curry powder
9 tablespoons flour
8 cups coconut milk

2 pounds boneless chicken thighs, cut into bite-sized pieces
6 ounces white wine or dry vermouth
3 tablespoons peanut oil
Salt and pepper to taste
6 tablespoons curry powder

Sauté garlic, ginger, and onion in clarified butter. Add salt, sugar, curry powder, and flour. Mix thoroughly. Add coconut milk a little at a time, stirring to a smooth thickness, and cook for 20 minutes until sauce begins to boil. Allow to stand several hours. Strain before using.

Marinate chicken in white wine or dry vermouth and peanut oil. Add pinch of salt and pepper. Let stand 15 minutes. Pan fry curry powder in saucepan. Add marinated chicken. When chicken is cooked, pour in curry sauce.

Note: Pictured is The Willows Curry with chicken which can be substituted for shrimp.

Firehouse Stuffed Chicken Thighs

Submitted by Mark Kuwaye

I am one of a team of Fire Captains at Honolulu's busiest stations, Pāwa'a Fire Station near Don Quixote. A firefighter's day is unpredictable; on any given day we may have up to 100 calls.

When I signed up in 1990, my job description listed fire fighting and prevention, driving apparatus, operating pumps and aerial ladders. The word "cook" was not part of that description. Nevertheless, we work 24-hour shifts and cooking for your crew is mandatory, whether you've honed your culinary skills or not. It's a requirement!

Some firefighters come to the station with their own repertoire of recipes they have practiced on their families and friends. Quite a few of us skim the local cookbooks for ideas. We have a few winners that could stand next to Sam Choy or Emeril Lagasse. Those dinners are very popular—food fit for kings. Others just wing it. Usually the seasoned team members assist them. The process starts with a simple recipe that they'd like to eat, then grocery shopping to choose the choicest produce. There is a reason we are often in groups shopping together, and that is to share our acquired know-how, preparation skills, and short cuts.

We pick up recipes from fellow firefighters and regularly develop them to fit our tastes. We all come from different backgrounds and cultures and bring our own food experiences, ranging from Japanese to Hawaiian, Mexican to Jamaican. For myself, my mom, Norma Kuwaye, and my mom-in-law, Tomiko Nakasone, were great role models. If they cooked something I really enjoyed, they shared their recipe and their time to prepare it with me from beginning to end.

Serves 4 to 6

1/2 pound bacon, thinly sliced
1/2 large onion, diced
3 cans chicken broth, divided in half
1 large carrot, grated
2 stalks celery, diced
2 cloves garlic, smashed
1 block butter
1 box Stove Top stuffing
4 to 6 slices of sweet bread, diced in 1-inch pieces
1 can olives, chopped into rings
8 to 10 pieces skinless boneless thighs
Salt, to taste
Pepper, to taste
1 can cream of mushroom soup
1 teaspoon Kitchen Bouquet
Cornstarch to thicken gravy

To make the stuffing, in a medium skillet, fry bacon till crispy, add onion, cook until golden brown. Add 1-1/2 cans broth, carrot, celery, garlic, and butter. Bring to boil, then simmer for 10 minutes. Remove from stove. Add Stove Top stuffing and bread, toss together gently. Then add olives.

Preheat oven to 325°F.

Butterfly chicken thighs then season with salt and pepper to taste on both sides. Portion accordingly and spoon stuffing on chicken thigh then roll (toothpicks can be used to secure). Place open side down on baking sheet for 45 minutes to an hour. Check for doneness. Remove from oven.

Meanwhile, to make the gravy, use the same pot (don't wash) from stuffing mix and add remaining chicken broth, cream of mushroom soup, Kitchen Bouquet, and any leftover chicken (chopped up).

Spoon drippings from pan into gravy pot and bring gravy to boil and thicken with cornstarch as necessary.

Note: You can substitute the chicken with pork, chicken, or Portugese sausage. You can also use wheat bread instead of sweet bread.

Okinawan Pig's Feet Soup

Submitted by Lance Shimabuku, Rainbow Drive-In

I struck gold the day I accepted the general manager's position at Kapahulu Avenue's well-known Rainbow Drive-In. Both President Harvey Iwamura and Vice President Jim Gusukuma are down-to-earth, good-hearted gentlemen. The family atmosphere they created is reflected in the list of long-term employees. All the team members enjoy being together as one big ʻohana. Being part of this ʻohana reminds me of my own ʻohana, which is where my culinary education began.

My mom was a great cook and as a kid I used to enjoy watching her cook and helping her. The biggest event for our family was New Year's Eve, and our house was the gathering place. My mom prepared most of the dishes, which included maki sushi, nishime, konbu maki, shrimp and vegetable tempura, fried chicken, undagi and nantu. But the dish that everyone in the family looked forward to was prepared by my dad: Okinawan pig's feet soup.

He took pride in making this soup, from going to Chinatown and picking up the best-looking Island pig's feet, to cutting and preparing the vegetables the night before. Early the next morning, he would light up a charcoal grill to sear the pig's feet, which brings out the flavor and gives it a nice color. My job was to scrape off all the charred areas. He told me, "You need to learn this so you can carry on the tradition." Now, my father-in-law also makes an awesome pig's feet soup, so I took the best of the two dads' (George Shimabuku and Charles Okido) recipes and put it together to come up with this recipe.

Mom is no longer with us and Dad is no longer able to cook, but along with my wife, Diane, Uncle Eddie, and my two nephews, Len and Micah, I carry on this family tradition every year.

I joined Rainbow Drive-In because of their heart-warming family atmosphere. It's all about taking care of your ʻohana.

Serves 14

- 4 pieces pig's feet (long cut)
- 2 gallons water
- 1/4 pound ginger, peeled and crushed
- 20 pieces dried shiitake mushrooms, soaked and cut in quarters
- 4 tablespoons hon dashi
- 4 ounces nishime konbu, soaked to soften, tied in knots and cut (nishime-style)
- 3 pounds daikon
- 6 pounds togan
- Salt to taste
- 3 bunches mustard cabbage, cut, blanched, cooled in ice water and drained

Sear pig's feet over an open-flame grill. Make sure it is seared well on all sides. Don't be afraid if it gets charred. Place in a large bowl of cool water and with a paring knife, scrape charred areas. Rinse, cut in pieces, place in a large pot (about 16 quarts) and add 2 gallons of water.

Bring to a boil, skim off impurities that rise, and simmer. Continue skimming occasionally. This will ensure a clear broth.

Add ginger, shiitake mushrooms, and dashi, and simmer for about 2 hours or until the pig's feet start becoming tender. Add konbu and daikon, bring to a boil and simmer.

After 20 minutes, add togan and bring to a boil again. Simmer for 20 minutes. Season with salt.

To serve, top each bowl of soup with some blanched mustard cabbage.

Dad's Shortrib Beef Stew

Submitted by Mona Chang Vierra

Grand Cafe & Bakery is a family affair! It was founded in 1923 by my grandfather, Mr. Ti Chong Ho, and his partner, Mr. Pang. Ti Chong Ho was born in the Kingdom of Hawai'i and lived to see his birthplace become the 50th State. His love of his family, quality food preparation and presentation inspired his family over the generations.

Eighty-one years later, in 2004, I reopened Grand Cafe & Bakery with my friend and business partner, Patsy Izumo. Within a year, my son, Anthony Kui Sin Vierra, took over the reins as Executive Chef. Patsy's grandson, Brandt Izumo, is a personable server, and my daughter, Jennifer, handles the research and development.

Patsy and I frequent Chinatown vendors to select fresh produce, fruit, and other delicacies. Chef Anthony recalls his Kung Kung—Yun Kui "Yankee" Chang—taking him and his sister grocery shopping in Chinatown. In fact, Dad's shortrib beef stew required a trip to Chinatown to visit our favorite butcher, Richard Chun, and his son, Howard, at the Old O'ahu Market—Ewa. Our request would be made and long strips of ribs would be brought out from the walk-in refrigerator. Once the right strips were selected, the butcher would cut and gently wipe the bone fragments from the pieces. Then he would bundle it in pink butcher paper for the trip home.

Serves 6 to 8

5 pounds short ribs, cut 1-inch thick
Salt and pepper
Flour for dredging
2 tablespoons oil
2 round onions, quartered
6 to 7 carrots, peeled and cut in 3/4- to 1-inch pieces
3 cans tomato sauce
3 potatoes, cut into large chunks

Salt and pepper the short ribs and dredge in flour.

Heat oil in a large pot, brown onions and ribs evenly. Once all pieces are browned, drain any excess oil and return ribs to pot. Add carrots and pour in tomato sauce, sprinkle excess flour over the mixture and add enough water to cover the carrots. Cover the pot. Bring to a boil. Reduce heat to low and simmer for 2 to 2-1/2 hours, stirring every 15 minutes so stew will not stick to the pot.

Add potatoes during the last 45 minutes. When cool, place in refrigerator. A day later, remove any oil that has formed on the top. Heat gently and serve over rice.

This beef stew remains one of our family favorites, and when prepared and served, it evokes warm, loving memories of our family!

Char Hung Sut

It's all in the family: Ti Chong Ho's wife, Kim Shee Mau, had a younger brother, Man Siu Mau, who married Bat Moi. She established the state's "must stop" dim sum location, Char Hung Sut in 1945.

The Chinese translation, "Fragrance of the Tea House," is the perfect description. The manapua, pork hash, mai tai soo, ip jai, taro cake, and rice cakes are packed and carried out by happy customers. Over the many years, the dim sum was a "must take home" to families and friends on neighbor islands, the mainland, and beyond. The recipes for the much-sought-after dim sum were hers and are still utilized today. This pleasant, strikingly beautiful woman continued to work diligently alongside her employees through her 80s. Her spirit remains strong through her children, grandchildren, and great-grandchildren, who have assumed the family tradition and business.

New Year's Day Korean Man Doo

**Submitted by Chef and Owner Kelvin Ro,
Diamond Head Market and Grill**

My Korean grandmother, my father's mother, used to make this man doo dish at our annual New Year's feast with other incredible Korean favorites like bulgogi, kalbi, and fish jun. All types of kim chee and various side dishes were served, including warabi, or fern shoots Korean-style, and soybean sprouts that were individually cleaned by taking the root off the end and made into namul (salad). There were a lot of New Year's traditions, and this dish was significant and eaten with the family during the holidays.

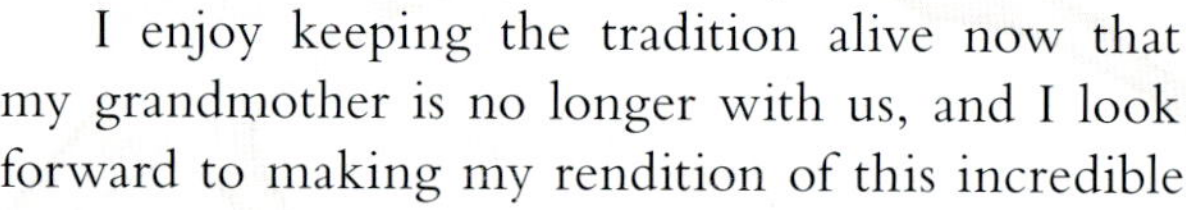

I enjoy keeping the tradition alive now that my grandmother is no longer with us, and I look forward to making my rendition of this incredible Korean dinner on New Year's Day. Grandma Ro usually prepped for a few days. We would arrive at her home in Wahiawā and help her make the man doo. I remember her adding different ingredients back then, but I've altered her recipe according to my personal taste.

Serves 4 to 6

2 cups kim chee cabbage, chopped and drained
2 cups firm tofu, chopped and drained
2 cups bean sprouts, blanched and chopped
1 pound ground pork (ground turkey can be substituted)
2 tablespoons sesame oil
1 tablespoon salt
1 teaspoon black pepper
2 tablespoons finely chopped garlic
2 tablespoons grated ginger
1 tablespoon shoyu
1 tablespoon koo chu jung sauce
1 teaspoon sugar
1/2 cup chopped green onion
Man doo wrappers (oval/round)

Dipping Sauce:

3/4 cup shoyu
1/4 cup sugar
1/4 cup water
1/2 cup vinegar
2 tablespoons ground Korean chili pepper sauce (koo chu jung) or kim chee sauce
2 tablespoons finely chopped green onion
2 tablespoons finely chopped cilantro
1 tablespoon ground toasted sesame seeds
1 teaspoon grated ginger
1 teaspoon finely chopped garlic
1 tablespoon sesame seed oil

Finely chop the kim chee cabbage, tofu, and bean sprouts, and squeeze water out with a cheese cloth until dry. Add pork and rest of the ingredients and mix well.

Put a teaspoonful of mix onto a man doo wrapper and brush water on the edges. Fold in half to close into a half moon and crimp edges tight. Boil, deep-fry, or pan-fry for 4 minutes, or until done.

Mix all sauce ingredients together. Serve man doo with Dipping Sauce.

You can eat this traditionally with a homemade chicken broth that has been clarified and garnished with chopped scrambled egg, sliced nori, shredded chicken, sliced green onion, and a dash of toasted ground sesame seeds. You can also eat this as an appetizer without the broth, deep-fried or pan fried, like gyoza. You can alter any of the ingredients to your personal taste. Enjoy!

Refrigerator Potato Rolls

Submitted by Chef Mark Okumura

Making refrigerator potato rolls was always memorable because of the aroma that only bread making can produce. The smell of the yeast while the rolls were rising in the bedroom, where it was nice and warm with the windows closed, then the aroma of the fresh rolls in the oven being baked, is just unforgettable! We made these for years, but one year we tried something new since Grandpa had a sweet tooth. This roll recipe evolved into anpan using tsubushi-an, a prepared sweetened azuki bean paste, which is stuffed into the rolls.

Makes 3 dozen

1 cup mashed potato
1/2 cup potato water, lukewarm
1 package active dry yeast
2/3 cup butter
2/3 cup sugar
2 teaspoons salt
1 cup milk, scalded
2 eggs, beaten
6 to 7 cups all-purpose flour, sifted
Butter for greasing and brushing

Peel, cube, and boil 1 large russet potato until soft. Reserve 1/2 cup potato water. Mash the potato and measure 1 cup.

Cool potato water to lukewarm and dissolve the yeast in it.

In a large mixing bowl combine the mashed potato, butter, sugar, salt, and hot milk. Cool. Stir in beaten eggs and dissolved yeast.

Stir in flour with a wooden spoon and mix it until a soft dough develops. Gently knead and form the dough into a ball and place in a buttered bowl. Turn over to butter top, cover well, and refrigerate dough overnight.

Two hours before baking, remove dough from refrigerator and let temper about 1 hour. Then pinch walnut-size pieces off and roll into balls. Place on buttered baking pans 2 inches apart.

Cover with a dish cloth and place in a warm, draft-free area to proof and rise until double in size.

Bake in a 375 to 400°F preheated oven for 20 minutes until golden brown. Brush with butter if desired.

Option: To make anpan, flatten ball and add 1 tablespoon of prepared tsubushi-an into center of each dough roll and seal on bottom. Place on buttered pans and follow directions for rolls.

Corn on the Cob, Japanese-Style

(Toomorokoshi no Teriyaki)

Submitted by Jade Ogoshi

Toomorokoshi might be my favorite Japanese vocabulary word. It means corn, but to me it means temple festivals in Japan where huge ears of grilled teriyaki corn are sold for 500 yen. I finally discovered how to recreate this dish with the ultra-sweet, ultra-crisp corn grown by Rob Nozawa and his family in Kahuku. Rob and his sister, Stephanie, are fifth-generation farmers who work 70 acres of land with their parents, Jigger and Clarita.

Any around-the-island trek for our family requires a mandatory stop at the Nozawa roadside corn stand. Nozawa corn, when eaten in the field, leaves you smeared with juicy goodness—the same as devouring a perfectly ripe fruit. If you somehow manage to have your fill of unvarnished corn goodness, try this recipe with any leftovers.

Serves 4

4 ears corn

Glaze:
1/3 cup shoyu
1 tablespoon mirin or honey

Cook corn in boiling water until tender. Broil under broiler (toaster oven is more energy efficient); turn and brush with glaze. Or grill on the BBQ.

Mom Kodama's Brownie Recipe

Submitted by Ivy Nagayama

This is Mom's original recipe. She developed it through the many years of cooking and baking for her family. Mom always did everything whole-heartedly and was ALWAYS full of life and grace. She actually trained all of our Sansei chefs to make her recipe. Having this recipe and sharing it with others is like having Mom back here in our kitchens.

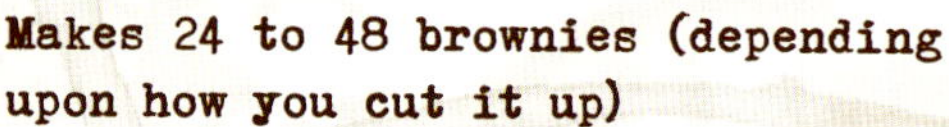
Makes 24 to 48 brownies (depending upon how you cut it up)

- 1-1/2 cups unsalted butter, at room temperature
- 2 cups cocoa powder
- 4 cups sugar
- 8 eggs, lightly beaten
- 3 cups flour
- 2 teaspoons baking powder
- 2 teaspoons salt
- 2 cups chopped nuts, any kind
- 1 cup macadamia nuts, chopped

Preheat the oven to 350°F. Butter a 12x18-inch jelly roll pan or a baking sheet with sides.

In a saucepan, combine the butter and cocoa powder over medium heat, stir until melted and combined.

In a large bowl, combine the sugar and eggs. Add the cocoa mixture and mix gently. Into another bowl, sift the flour, baking powder, and salt, and add—a little at a time—to the wet ingredients, mixing until incorporated.

Fold in the nuts.

Pour the batter into the prepared pan and bake for 30 minutes, checking periodically, until a toothpick inserted in the center comes out clean. Let cool, then cut into bars or squares.

We do a Mom Kodama's brownie Sundae by adding a scoop of vanilla ice cream topped with whipped cream, lots of chocolate sauce, and chopped macadamia nuts and a cherry.

Taro Cake
(Woo Tul Gow)

Submitted by Marion Wong

When my paternal grandmother, Chinn Chun Shee, arrived from China, she could not speak a word of English, but she sure could cook!

She often came to our home to cook for us. Grandmom was eager to pass along her recipes. I watched her intently as she prepared the dishes that are part of my recipe list today. She would use teacups or bowls to measure her ingredients—an unconventional method of measuring, but it made sense to her. We used a great deal of sign language to communicate. I eventually translated all her recipes into standard cups and measuring spoons for my own use.

Our first restaurant was Leon's Tavern in Kailua, then in 1957 we opened Andy's Drive Inn. That was the beginning of our restaurant empire. My husband Andy and I expanded to Byron's Drive In, Wong's Okazuya, Byron's II, Coral Reef Restaurant at the Old Ala Moana Shopping Center, Chinese Chuckwagon, Orson's, Chowder House, Fishmonger's Wife, Seafood Emporium, Oink, then Andrew's. Between baking signature pies for the restaurants and shuttling the children to all their activities, those were the best years of my life. And during those years, Grandmom (even at 90 years old) helped with my six children and food preparation at home. Her English was still rough, but her mind was as sharp as a pin. She remembered all her great-grandchildren's names and birthdays, and she could recount stories about each of them. She was an exceptional woman.

I always tell my children that many recipes are good, but if you include the extra "love" in the preparation, it just tastes better!

recipe continued on page 190

Makes 4 (8-inch) cakes

- 1 cup flour
- 1 cup water or chicken broth
- 1/2 cup roast pork, diced
- 1/4 cup char siu, diced
- 1/2 cup dried shrimp
- shoyu to taste
- 1 small corm of Chinese taro, (approximately 1 pound) peeled and diced (see note)
- 2 teaspoons oil
- 3 tablespoons lam see (Chinese black olives) (reserve 1 tablespoon for garnish)
- 2 stalks green onion, sliced
- 2 teaspoons sesame seeds
- 1 egg, scrambled & fried, shredded

Combine flour and water, set aside. Dice then fry together roast pork, char siu, and dried shrimp. Add shoyu to taste. Set aside.

Peel taro with rubber gloves to avoid any skin irritation. Dice taro into 3/4-inch cubes. Fry taro in frying pan with oil, then cover and simmer for 15 minutes.

Add pork mixture, lam see, green onions, and flour mixture. Mix well. Salt to taste.

Grease four 8-inch pans and divide mixture evenly. Place in steamer and steam for 25 minutes.

Garnish with lam see, sesame seeds, and shredded eggs.

Note: Chinese taro is dry land taro. Wear rubber gloves when handling raw taro. The outer skin of the taro causes skin irritation. Cook well.

Grandma's Shortbread Cookies

Submitted by Jeanie Wyss

Grandma Kumeko (Kay) Hayashi Fujii was born in Hawi, Hawai'i on a sugar plantation. She was the ninth of 11 children. Although she was a good student, she was forced to quit school after the sixth grade to work in the sugar cane fields to help with the family finances. In her teenage years, she worked for more prominent families as a house helper, where she learned to cook dishes that the family enjoyed. Scottish shortbread cookies was one of the many recipes she continued to use throughout her life. She made many people happy with these cookies.

Makes 32 cookies

- 2 cups butter
- 1 cup sugar
- 4 cups flour
- 1/2 teaspoon lemon extract (optional)
- Lots of love

Mix butter, sugar, and flour until very, very fluffy. Add lemon extract. Mix well.

Put batter in a 10x17-inch jelly roll pan. Pat down to make dough level. Press down edges so that it is a tiny bit lower than the surface of dough. You can use the handle end of a fork that is dusted with a little flour.

Using fork tines dipped in flour, make holes on the whole sheet of batter. Bake at 325°F for about 45 to 60 minutes or until light brown. Cut as soon as you remove pan from oven. Cool.

Pumpkin Chiffon Pie

Submitted by Chef Mark Okumura

Thanksgiving and Christmas lunches were always celebrated at Grandpa's house in Wahiawā with the Yamada family. It was always a big deal going to Wahiawā from town back then without the freeway systems now in place. I used to think that it was so far away.

Grandpa enjoyed growing and raising all kinds of plants and animals. He would always grow a lot of fruits, vegetables, and flowers in the back. I remember feeding the turkeys in the coop not realizing until years later that they were going to be on the buffet table for our feasts.

Grandma was a great cook and handed down recipes to my mother, which she taught to me. Unfortunately, Grandma suffered a stroke when I was young, so I was not able to learn a lot from her directly. This recipe for pumpkin chiffon pie is one I have made through the years and continue to cherish. As far back as I can remember, we've only eaten pumpkin chiffon pie for Thanksgiving. I remember one year when someone brought a regular pumpkin pie to the party. I thought that it was so strange because we never had anything like that before.

Makes 2 (10-inch or 9-inch) pies

2 packages + 2 teaspoons gelatin
1/2 cup water
2-1/2 cups solid packed pumpkin purée
2 cups granulated sugar, divided
8 large eggs, separated
1/2 teaspoon ground nutmeg
1/2 teaspoon ground cinnamon
1/2 teaspoon ground ginger
1 cup evaporated milk
1/2 teaspoon salt
2 (10-inch or 9-inch) pre-baked pie shells
Fresh whipped cream or whipped topping

Dissolve and bloom the gelatin in water and set aside.

Combine pumpkin, 1 cup sugar, egg yolks, nutmeg, cinnamon, ginger, and evaporated milk in a medium saucepot over medium-high heat. Stirring constantly with a rubber spatula, bring to a boil and remove immediately from heat.

recipe continued on page 194

Add gelatin mixture, stir to dissolve, and combine thoroughly.

Transfer cooked mixture to a stainless steel bowl and place over an ice bath to cool, stirring occasionally until cool, but not set.

While cooked mixture is cooling, make a meringue by whipping the egg whites with the salt until foamy. Gradually add the remaining 1 cup sugar slowly and whip until firm peaks form.

Fold 1/3 of the meringue into the cooled pumpkin mixture to lighten it, then gently fold this into the remaining meringue until thoroughly combined and mixture is streak-free and well blended, being careful not to deflate volume.

Gently fill the pre-baked pie shells by mounding the filling into the shells. Smooth the tops of the fillings and refrigerate overnight or for at least 4 hours to set before serving.

Serve with fresh whipped cream or whipped topping, if desired.

Crispy Waffles

Submitted by Justin Tanioka, Tanioka's Seafood & Catering

One month before the opening of our family's business in Waipahu, I was born. My mom had her hands full with me. During those preschool years, I remember running around the rice cookers with my grandmoms in tow. My mom and dad, Lynn and Mel Tanioka, built Tanioka's Seafoods and Catering with humble beginnings together with friends and family at their side. Grandmom Tanioka, now retired, managed, cooked, and assembled many of the specialty dishes we offer. Still today, Grandmom Furukawa helps with the catering coordination. My Aunty Esther Ringor is the all-around person helping out at the counter, cooking, or whatever else needs to be done. My parents' motto—quality food with a friendly smile—is a reflection of who we have become today.

On Sundays, we gather at home, Mom with ladle in hand and Dad sipping his Kona coffee and keeping her company. Cooking together is what they love best. One of our favorite dishes is this crispy waffle with lots of butter and syrup. Their grandson, Ethan, lights up when he's served the first piping hot waffles out of the iron. The butter liquefies as soon as it hits the steam from the waffles.

Please enjoy these crispy, melt-in-your-mouth waffles with your family!

Serves 4

2 cups Bisquick
1 egg
1/2 cup vegetable oil
1-1/3 cups club soda, chilled

Preheat waffle iron on medium-high heat.

In a medium bowl, whisk together all ingredients. Do not overmix batter.

Spray a non-stick oil on the inside surface of the waffle iron. Pour batter into the iron to cover the surface of the iron. Cover and wait until golden brown, approximately 5 minutes. Serve immediately with butter and maple syrup.

Recipe Index

Index

Calling all home cooks!

Are you willing to share your secret recipes? If so, we want to hear from you. Tell us your recipe's story for our next cookbook. How did your culinary interests begin? Anyone inspire or mentor you? What role does your recipe play in your everyday family life—is it something you enjoy often, was it handed down from a family member, is it a popular dish that's often requested at parties?

Send your recipe to info@mutualpublishing.com, attention Gay Wong.

Be a part of Hawai'i's community table of culinary treasures.